One Journey

A travelogue of awakening

Michael Forester

PARALIGHT

PRESS

First published in Great Britain in 2018
by Paralight Press

www.michaelforester.co.uk

The right of Michael Forester to be identified as author of
this work has been asserted by him in accordance with the
Copyright, Designs and Patents Act 1988

ISBN: 978-0-9955248-7-3

Cover Image © Michael Forester
Internal Images © Michael Forester

Printed and bound by TJ International, Padstow, Cornwall

"An unputdownable travelogue that asks many questions for which the answers are complex. As good as Michael Forester's award winning *If It Wasn't For That Dog!*"

Millie Adams – author of The Waterway Girls series

Flash in the Pan

An ethereal vicissitude ferments anticipation;
strews molting tufts of coalescing consciousness
across the beckoning portals of yestermorrow.

She has morning eyes,
This Grace;
This Essence;
This Familiar,

crystalising awareness
from the cooling mud pools
of primeval monotony;

chipping at the jagged corners
with flint chisels of mortality;

patiently panning the silt
of past life patterns.

Elevated to this windswept crag,
I can see clear across the valley of this incarnation
and on into the next.

South Africa: Table Mountain towards Oudekraal

Contents

Preface

There is only one Journey and it is travelled on the road to enlightenment. We commence it the moment we enter the physical world, and complete it the moment we leave.

At times we walk in the company of other wayfarers, at times alone. But always, we travel with ourselves, for our journey is travelled on a road of self-discovery.

However, our exploration is not exclusively introspective. In seeking to discover more of who we are, our attention is focussed as much outward as it is inward. For often, our outer ventures are a metaphor and reflection of our inner Journey. And all such voyages, undertaken sequentially, connect into one great gestalt of the soul.

Here are four voyages, ventures undertaken simultaneously into the soul and into the outer world, undertaken over a period of fourteen years:

A confrontation with the devastation of the Amazon rainforest and the unceasing exploitation of its resources and people.

An encounter with the power of forgiveness in South Africa, fifteen years after the ending of apartheid.

A pilgrimage of self-exploration and enlightenment to Nepal and the Himalayas.

A learning and teaching tour of the Philippines, evaluating the impact of rapid economic modernisation.

I have taken each trip to discover more of myself by exploring more of the world that is around me. I share these journeys with you with the intention of adding illumination to your own journey.

Travel far; travel deep; travel wisely.
Namaste.

Michael Forester, October 2018

Rain Forest

Having awoken spiritually in the millennium year, I spent some four years exploring my connection with a newfound reality, documenting the learning in a previous book, Forest Rain. Though during these years, I had travelled away from my home in the UK, my first long-distance venture of exploration took place at the end of 2004, to South America. I spent two weeks travelling through Chile, Argentina and Brazil before embarking on the deeper purpose of my visit: to experience first-hand the Amazon rainforest in order to understand both more of its significance to whole-earth ecology, and how it and the people who live there are being exploited, mercilessly. This is what I found.

Day 1: Rio to Rain

I am told, there is a first time for everything. This is the first time I have ever sat down to write by candlelight on damp paper. I'm pretty sure it is also the first time I have stayed in a hotel room with no electricity or hot water. What a creature of comfort I have become, attuned to a mode of living that was unusual as recently as in the time of my grandparents' youth. My friend Penny observed by e-mail some days ago that a trip to the Amazon rainforest would stretch my comfort zones. How right she has proved to be.

I flew into Manaus from Rio de Janeiro on Saturday, a five-hour trip including a brief touchdown in Brasilia. The airport is another monotonous collection of flight gates, bilingual notices and baggage carousels. Waiting for me as I emerged, travel-shocked, into yet another anonymous arrivals hall was my guide, Elcio, an Amazonian Indian of the Mundurucu tribe. Don't let that conjure up images of blowpipes and cannibals round the pot. Dressed in the virtually regulation t-shirt and shorts as required by the climate, Elcio is a man of about forty, just a little shorter than my own five foot nine and with a waistline that rivals my own. He's a former electronics engineer and a speaker of at least four languages to my certain knowledge – probably more. He switched to being a tour guide ten years ago because it pays better.

In our air-conditioned minibus, we collect the rest of the party (a young Italian couple with limited English and an even younger Swiss couple with virtually no inclination to speak to someone of my age in any language at all), and head out through the suburbs of Manaus towards the river. We're effectively in the centre of the South American continent here, with rainforest stretching endlessly in all directions. The one means of transport that has permitted this city to be built at all, is the river itself. So, I look around me at dual carriageways, coffee shops, shanty villages and an endless stream of Volkswagen Beetles (they never went out of production here), and realise that this city, buried as it is in the heart of the Amazon jungle, is actually like any other in the Third World – hot, dusty, bustling with street corner commerce and bursting with people that have never known, and never will know, the luxuries of privileged existence of which I avail myself daily. I am already embarrassed by my wealth.

Initially, at least, Elcio has little to say to me. The young couples at the front of the minibus are closer to him and easier to talk to, rattling on in Italian, which, I am later informed, is similar to Portuguese. He does make a point of telling me in English, though, that the jungle lodge we are bound for has no electricity, no telephones and no Internet access. I find myself wondering how I will fare on this vacation of challenges, with no one to talk to and a rapidly shrinking level of comfort.

After perhaps thirty minutes' drive on good quality tarmacked urban roads, we eventually pass under some enormous arches, where the industrial buildings start to die slowly away like cries on the wind. The paved roads concede to uneven pot-holed concrete, and the factories and offices yield to canvass-roofed street-side stalls, selling local fruit and tourist trinkets.

We appear to be arriving at the Amazon itself, though for the largest river in the world and a pivotal element in the global eco-structure, it is singularly unassuming in its announcement of its presence. If I had given the matter thought, based on the modern city I have just left behind me, I might have expected to see up-to-date jetties and docking facilities, bills of lading and business hotels. But there is none of this. The broken concrete road drops sharply down to the river, where worn-out landing ramps on lorry-sized wheels dip their toes cautiously in the muddy water, as if afraid they will contract metal fatigue from something malevolent, lurking silently under the brown waves.

My first glimpse of the river is no more encouraging. It is wide, light brown and highly industrialised, judging by the container ships anchored in the middle, perhaps half a mile away. Such vessels penetrate with ease to the heart of the continent through this aquatic artery that pumps the lifeblood of the planet so unassumingly. The rain is falling as if someone upended an ocean over us (not for nothing do they call this the rainforest) and everyone in the vicinity has already dived for cover. We wait in the minibus for it to ease off a little, and I gaze nonchalantly on the unmanned trinket stalls, each now separated from its neighbour by rivulets cascading down towards the river.

Eventually, the downpour recedes a little and the sky clears. It is like that here – an hour of torrential deluge that you can't keep out of your clothes, then, it suddenly disappears as if it never was. We step carefully towards the river, trying to avoid treading ankle deep into the streams that are still hurtling down through the mud and make our way to the boat that will take us forward on our journey. Locals carry our bags on their shoulders. I've been told to bring only five kilos of luggage with me. Later, I will discover why.

The rainforest is aptly named

Was it a mistake to come here? I'm beginning to think it might have been. I'm not aware of it at this moment, but an invasive negativity has been rising around me like flood water since I left Rio – in fact, from the time I started focussing on coming to the rainforest.

For my short stay in Rio itself, my guide had been Vera, a middle-aged Brazilian woman with a pronounced German accent. As her last duty, she had shepherded me out to the airport for the flight to Manaus at seven in the morning. Our conversation had primarily concerned the economics of this poor, struggling country. Brazil changed its currency to the Real in 1993, since which time it has stabilised, she had said. Now, with the decline in interest rates since the millennium and, more recently, the fall in the value of the US dollar in 2003, the country stands a real chance of getting out from under the mountain of debt that has so debilitated it and prolonged the poverty of its citizens, not least those three hundred and sixty thousand street children that live rough in Rio. Numbers like these and problems of this scale are virtually beyond my comprehension, let alone my ability to affect them. So, I had changed the subject and tentatively asked Vera about deforestation. She had drawn back visibly, mumbling something about the forest being too big to police and the fault lying with the Asians who had already deforested their own continent and now had come to do the same illegally in Brazil. I had broken eye contact with her, embarrassed, and drifted into silence, not wishing to offend her. She is, after all, only one individual and as we all know, one individual can do little about the foreboding, anonymous 'them'. But I had realised I had touched on a national raw nerve, and like a half-noticed irritation that grows to a throbbing insistent ache, the pain is not going to go away.

So, now, I find myself climbing aboard a sixty-foot double-deck river boat, one of dozens that ferry passengers up and down the Amazon to and from the city, and feel the darkness of this negativity seeping like ink on blotting paper across my mind and my emotions. As I become gradually aware of these angry and depressed thoughts, I am confused. It is almost five months since I entered into daily meditation and committed myself to the proactive elimination of negativity from my thinking. I have seen benefit beyond words from doing so, these last months. Yet, now, darkness is intruding systematically and pervasively, deeper and deeper into my silent, serene places. Doubts about the wisdom of the trip cede to anger over the low amenity of the facilities to be afforded, which gives way to self-criticism for so feeling, in a progressive gestalt that blows dark rain clouds across the clear blue sky of my mind. I am at a loss to identify the cause of these unwanted thoughts and feelings. Surely, such simple and short-lived inconveniences cannot be responsible for this profound and pervasive depression washing over me? It will be another twenty-four hours before I become aware of the true cause of my debilitating inner state.

Into the rainforest by motorised canoe

We chug our way downriver, passing the point where the stark black waters of the Rio Negro join the more muted brown currents of the Rio Solimones at the official beginning of the Rio Amazonas. I cast my eyes around at much industrialisation and muse again upon the thought that everything has to be imported into this green wilderness – the road stone, the oil, the food, manufactured goods or at least, their raw materials. Virtually everything is alien to the locality. I wonder what it is that the Amazon has to offer in exchange for all the imported trappings of modern life. Elcio tells me that it is electronics. There are over five hundred electronics factories here, for the Brazilian government has declared the area a free port. The companies that operate here pay no taxes, and they have descended upon the region like shoppers on a shoe sale. He says that it is rumoured that Microsoft will come here soon. He is grateful, since prosperity will follow wherever Microsoft leads.

As the diesel engines push us forward downriver, Elcio tells us that we will need to transfer to a canoe for the next leg of our journey, because the waters will become too shallow for a vessel of this size. From my childhood diet of old colonial movies, I visualise natives with bones through their noses paddling furiously, while bearers carry our luggage on their shoulders (and hence the five kilo limit). But of course the canoe is motorised, its outboard connected to the propeller by a long metal stem, so as to permit the boat to pass through waters little deeper than its own draft. And the weight limit has been imposed because of the size of the canoe. Despite my ignorance, the twenty-first century has arrived in the Amazon, whether the rainforest wants it or not.

Having switched into the canoe at a small floating transfer station, we make our way upstream along one of the innumerable tributaries of the river. Elcio points out dead trees in the river. "Termites," he says. Once upon a time the anteaters kept the termite numbers down. Then, weekend hunters, outsiders from Manaus, came and the anteaters were ridiculously easy prey. As their numbers declined, so the termite colonies grew beyond their design level in the system, feasting on the bark until the trees died. It is my first lesson on the effects of imbalance in the eco-structure created by the thoughtless intervention of those who know little of the dynamic equilibrium of the rainforest. There will be many more lessons to come in these next three days. And I am to learn that the better part of my reason for coming here is bound up with seeing more clearly, much more clearly than I could ever do at home, that all of our ecosystem, all of our world, functions upon the foundation of a sensitive, balanced exchange of energy. The forest is commencing my education.

Elcio tells me it is rainy season. I have no difficulty believing him as the skies empty upon us once more. "But when does the river rise?" I ask.

"From now until April," he answers. "But it used to rise three metres, and now it is less. And it is the same with the rain. It does not come as it used to in rainy season, then, ceasing in dry season." Now, the area is subject to storms and lightning and unexpected flooding. There are great swathes of land, deep inside the rainforest, that have been devastated by lightning. The forest peoples say that the sky is angry at the forest. I think not. It seems to me that it is the forest that is angry; angry and depressed at the abominable way in which it is being raped and abused by the never-ending onslaught of outsiders that penetrate it, uninvited and unwelcomed, and who do not know its Tao.

Rainforest e-mail: beat on a tree

Finally, the canoe draws up to a small wooden jetty where we disembark, porters once again disappearing into the distance with our bags. There is a few minutes' walk to the lodge hotel, which will be home for the next three nights. "Why," I enquire of Elcio, "was it built so far from the river?"

"It wasn't," comes the answer. "It is built at the high water point." This is some four hundred metres or so from the low water point at which we have alighted from the boat. I am beginning to understand how everything in this region has to account for the breathing of the river, its inhalation and exhalation taking it from low water to high and back again each year.

A few minutes' walk over dusty paths and bridges brings us to the lodge, built with rich red mahogany floors, palm leaf roofs, and almost no walls in the public areas. It is lit in the late afternoon twilight by gaslight. Later, I hear the sound of a rushing mighty wind. Intrigued, I go in search of the source. From somewhere deep in my memory of religious children's camps, I recall the term 'hurricane lamp'.

We dine in semi-darkness, or so it seems to eyes more used to neon and halogen. Food is simultaneously familiar and different. Chicken and beef combined with vegetables and fruits I cannot name. The young Italian couple, Massimiliano and Danila, make conversation in limited English. I am embarrassed that I can say nothing in Italian except "No palliano Italiano." Though we are without sufficient common language to make the conversation anything more than superficial, their hearts are warm and that is enough. After dinner, though it is still early, I head for bed. I have been travelling almost twelve hours. I fall asleep to the noise of the frogs calling to one another across the darkness. It is like the sound of one hollow wooden tube beaten against another. Darkness, it seems, invites no silence in the rainforest.

And yes, I am still angry.

Not all the wildlife is so wild

Day 2: Destruction of the Indispensible

I awake to yet more jungle sounds – parrots screeching in the trees, insects that sound like dive bombers. Being deafened, I can normally hear nothing without my hearing aids, which I remove for sleep. I imagine the volume as it sounds to fully functioning ears! I turn on the dim, battery-operated lamp, which yields perhaps twenty watts of light.

Then, I brace myself to shower in cold water. We may be almost on the equator, but the water is still shockingly cold. It reminds me of the showers I used to endure at school. I had promised myself when I left that I would never take a cold shower again. Evidently, it is time to reconsider.

Then, I turn to meditation, where I ponder my strange emotional state, for I have woken as lacking in equilibrium as I was when I had fallen asleep. Though there are no answers yet, I am mindful of the Buddhist approach to emotion, acknowledging it for what it is and being aware that it is not who and what I am. In so doing, the emotion passes. I breakfast on exotic fruit, sausage and egg that are eerily reminiscent of home. The morning's agenda is a walk in the jungle (growth between five and fifty years of age) and the rainforest (fifty to five hundred years, maybe more). We trek out from the hotel area, intrepid explorers in pursuit of the unknown (not!), stopping frequently for Elcio to explain the flora and fauna, and the uses to which it can be put. This reed is good for basket making, while that palm leaf will last four years as roofing to a house. Here is a tree that yields sap-like creamy milk. The Indians harvest it early in the morning before the heat of the day causes it to rise up the tree trunk. Once they have taken what they need, they pack soil onto the incision in the trunk, so as to ensure the tree comes to no harm. But the same sap is also used in the production of diabetic chewing gum. And the companies that manufacture it are not nearly so respectful of their place within the equilibrium of the eco-structure. They milk the sap in such a way that the tree often dies. The attitude is 'never mind, there are plenty more trees in the forest, and anyway, they're free, aren't they?' Commerce takes without replenishing. Here is a Caesar tree, the most expensive wood in the rainforest. It is maybe two hundred and fifty years old and now rare, particularly, around the river. 'They' send in helicopters, sever the tree at the base and lift it away for processing somewhere. Nothing is returned to the system, and the removal of the tree kills perhaps a thousand other plants that lived under its protection. Caesar has almost gone. Though he still reigns here for the present, how much longer can this rain last?

Elcio is telling me now that the South American rainforest produces 43% of the world's oxygen. Yet, in the last ten years alone, some 23% of it has been cut down for the one-off benefit of the sale of wood that took hundreds of years to grow. I am later to hear other estimates that are a little lower, though comparably consequential. The land is largely useless after the trees have gone, turning to sand. I shudder and think of the Sahara desert. Did some ancient generation fail to understand the place of another rainforest in the dynamic equilibrium of the eco-structure? And, are the sands of time running fast through the hourglass of ignorant deforestation for this rainforest, on which our supply of 'free' breathable air depends?

After our speaking-without-words last evening, Massimiliano and Danila are more conscious of me this morning, as I am of them. Danila in particular, is solicitous of me, turning to ensure I have a sense of being included in the group even if I cannot understand the language. Her concern is touching and I feel valued. To bridge a language gap with kindness and smiles is so easy, yet so infrequently done.

Elcio milks a tree without damage

Elcio's story unfolds at stop after stop, plant after plant, almost to the point of monotony. In location after location, I am shown the comparison between the attitude of the indigenous population who know they are part of the eco-structure and consequently live by the rules of replenishment, and that of the thick-skinned, insensitive ignorance of the invaders who live by different rules – the rules of taking what is there and is not 'charged for' by some other 'owner', for all 'they' know is the rule of self-interest. He tells us that Viagra, for instance, was developed from secrets known to the Amazonian Indians, but the world's enhanced virility has not resulted in a respectful return of energy to the locality in the building of a school, or the replanting of a devastated area. Malaria tablets were developed from a tea made by the Indians from a combination of forest plants. But when the secret was taken away by the drug companies and millions were subsequently made, nothing was paid in recognition of that profit, nor of the countless non-local lives saved by the drugs.

First, I grow quiet, then embarrassed at the ignorance of the culture from which I originate, then sad, then despairing, and finally, angry, until at last, I understand my emotional change on coming here, for I feel the despair and anger of this place itself. It is benevolent and loving beyond words, freely giving of its own substance to sustain life, all life, our life. And slowly, like the termites that chewed through the logs in the river, we burrow around inside it and tear away at its life force. No one seems to take ownership of this problem and its consequences. No one seems to want to take responsibility for stopping or preventing it. For days, leading up to this visit, my spirit guides have been impressing on me thoughts of this concept of dynamic equilibrium of the universe – always in motion, yet always in balance – until I see that everything that exists is in perpetual motion towards equilibrium, for that is the nature of existence. That, indeed, is the Tao.

However, we cannot long go on tearing away at the equilibrium of the eco-structure on which our own existence depends, for the system always returns to balance eventually, whatever the consequences for any one part of it, ourselves included. In anger, I wonder if we will have uprooted the last tree from the last forest, destroyed the last oxygenating plant, desecrated the last area of natural, productive beauty, before we see, as Joni Mitchell said back in the 1970s, that we have "paved paradise, put up a parking lot".

Yes, the rainforest is depressed. Yes, it is angry. And yes, I have sensed and absorbed its anger at its own violation. Yes, I want it to stop. Yes, I want all of us to realise the insanity of what we are doing, the folly of our actions that unbalance the equilibrium of the system on which our existence is a mere parenthetic contingency. 'They', the destroyers, are faceless and nameless. There is nowhere for me to vent my anger, which is why it has turned inwards as it has. Yes, I am angry, angry with 'them' and no, I do not know what to do about it.

An uncomfortable way of sleeping?

It is afternoon and we are scheduled to visit a local village to see rubber trees and learn more about local society. But on the way to the river, we take a detour. We walk first past my own room on the hotel campus, where Elcio points out the high water point to which the river rose in 1989, lapping at the steps up to the room. It comes as no surprise now, when he says that it has never risen as high again in the intervening fifteen years. Each summer, it has risen from November to May, but each high point has been just a little lower than the last. Now, our detour takes us past a local homestead. We are all endeared by the four-toed sloths the family keep as pets, and there is much clicking of electronic cameras, much cooing and aahing and stroking of fur. The nonchalant creature tolerates all this, more, it seems, with resignation than enjoyment, while continuing to chew on fruit as if we were not there. A second sloth is sleeping, hanging upside down from a tree branch, hunched limbs holding it apparently precariously in place. There have to be more uncomfortable ways of sleeping, but off-hand I can't think of any.

I look around the homestead and am conscious of being confronted by more poverty than I have ever encountered before. No one looks starved, and every child is clothed, save for shoes, which are of limited relevance in this environment. But there is an overwhelming sense of 'have not' about the place. Guiltily, I realise that this family, and everyone like it in the vicinity, lives daily without the electricity I am having to do without for a mere three days: no fridge, no TV, and they wouldn't even know what a microwave or the Internet was, no electric light; night after night, year after year. I find myself wondering what these people think of the strange groups of foreigners that have come from so far away to see them – people with wealth that to them is inestimable. They do not seem envious. Danila plays with a baby for a few moments. The nineteen-year-old mother of this child and two others does not grudge the smiles her baby freely bestows on the privileged strangers. Any moment now, we will walk out of her life of lack and back into opulence, casting no backward glance, bereft of the first idea of how to change this quirk of fate that makes us wealthy and her poor. Yet, I am reminded again that that which joins us is bigger than that which separates us. These people are my brothers and my sisters, my mother and my father, my sons and my daughters. Is there nothing I can do for them but stand by helplessly, while the robber barons, having denuded the natural resources of their own corners of the world, now turn their greedy eyes towards the little that these have-nots of the Amazon enjoy in their environment? The five Real I give to a little boy who has taken the trouble to show me his snake does nothing to relieve my battered conscience.

Elcio tells me that the first things children learn to do here are swim, paddle a canoe and spear fish. He is deeply frustrated at the virtual certainty that the children we have seen today will receive little or no education and will be unable to improve their lives economically beyond the subsistence level eked out by their parents. Poverty will cascade down through the generations like the rain that washes the sky and the land and the river.

A young rainforester on a floating home

I ask this multilingual electronics-engineer-turned-tour-guide why his own experience has been different from that of these children, for clearly Elcio is not just intelligent – he is also well educated. Somewhat reluctantly, he discloses to me that he is the youngest of fourteen children whose mother died when he was a year old. He had the fortune to be fostered with two doctors in Manaus, where he was raised and educated to First World standards. His older brothers and sisters did not fare so well in this respect, nor have their children. Elcio has started a school for the village from which he comes, he says, and sends materials and books monthly. Sadly, he adds that the government does little for them.

Sugar production in the rainforest

As we clamber aboard the canoe, I acknowledge silently that my anger has turned to a strange kind of frustrated thoughtfulness. For I am aware that the external energy which is desecrating the rainforest is also walking hand in hand with the energy that brings schools and hospitals. However limited the extent to which such institutions have so far touched the lives of local people, there is no doubting the fact that future health and prosperity will depend on more of such interventions, not fewer. The Yin that brings more hospitals and schools will mirror the Yang that takes away the trees and threatens worldwide devastation.

Yet, now, my thinking turns to the sheer imbalance of what is going on. The industrialised world is denuding the Amazon of its vast natural resources with an insane inattention to the consequences. At the same time, ludicrously, little energy is being put back into the region. Elcio says that no replanting is taking place to regenerate the forest taken, and that few schools and few hospitals touch the lives of the indigenous people in exchange for the wealth being ripped from the continent's heart. Worst of all, it appears to be no one's responsibility that this is happening. Not the Brazilian Government's, for they have their poor to feed from the legitimate sale of raw materials and have little manpower to police the deforestation of an area which is over two-and-a-half times the size of Europe; not the indigenous Indians, for they live naturally within the free exchange of the eco-structure, and have little short-term resistance to offer the thieves and plunderers; nor the rest of the world's, apparently, for there is, as yet, no such thing as a world government to police the desecration of a resource which even now is having universal consequence. Nor even the UN's, for reasons I cannot fathom. So, the destruction of a resource that produces some 43% of the world's oxygen is apparently no one's responsibility at all. Lemming-like, we determinedly throw ourselves over an eco-cliff, to dash ourselves on the rocks of slow suffocation below. Until each one of us is prepared to take ownership of this ludicrous devastation, nothing will change. Until you make it your problem and do something about it, nothing will change. Until I own up to the fact that it is my problem and act it, prevent it, nothing will change.

At dinner, Massimiliano and Danila ask what I have been writing, for today I have been jotting down notes of everything we have seen and done. When I tell them I am an author and try to explain the term 'Mind-Body-Spirit', I am pleasantly surprised to find that they understand. They are keen to see a copy of this book when it is finished, and to receive copies of my other books. I make a mental note to ensure that when this writing is done, I will send them the very first finished copy. I take Danila's hand and ask Massimiliano to explain to her my gratitude for the care she has shown me today. I have felt the energy she has offered me. Smiles all round confirm that the sentiment is understood, even if the words are not.

Day 3:   Fair Exchange

It is 4:10 am on the second full day of my visit here. As I did yesterday, I wake before the alarm and brave the cold shower water that my pampered flesh so dislikes. I turn next to meditation to ready myself for another day. Then, it's out to the hotel reception where we are meeting for a trip downriver to look for freshwater dolphins. I have not bothered with insect repellent this morning. Any self-respecting mosquito is still in bed at this hour – someone else's bed of course! As I close the door quietly on my room, the darkness of the jungle night wraps itself around me. With heavy cloud cover blotting out the moon and the stars, the only light comes from my little halogen torch. The forest is sleeping soundly now, the screeching and the knocking, the calling and the crying, subdued to sapient silence for a few short hours before dawn. Amidst our little group of six, I follow the beam of my torch down to the jetty, climbing into the canoe just as light begins to creep over the treetops. Minute by minute, as the sun rises invisibly behind the cotton wool clouds, the structure of the jungle emerges: now a skeleton etched onto X-ray film, now puffing and filling into monochrome substance. As the engine of the boat clanks wearily into life, we turn to open river. I try to capture the scene on photograph, but the light is insufficient to register on the electronic camera I carry. I give up and settle back to watch two forests emerge – the real one, looming dark and foreboding over the banks of the river, seemingly about to pounce on the other, its own reflection in the plate-glass mirror of perfectly still water. We carve a wedge through that stillness between the forests on either bank, severed like torn fur on some wild animal by the shining shard that is the river.

Yet, in reality, the river does little to tear the fabric of the forest, for the trees, though fewer in number here, step down into the water and stride into the centre, the trunks towering high above their own reflections, which double their length and grandeur. With none of us speaking, and only the engine throbbing at the back of the boat, we weave the thread of our wake through the foliage until we come to open water.

It is daylight now, though still a sanctified silent time that even the most immature members of our party seem reluctant to dismember with the giggles and cries that have characterised the last day or so. But for the pop-pop-popping of the two-stroke outboard, I am left to contemplate my own place, if any, in this silent grandeur.

As a world community, we apparently have yet to learn that the existence of our race is contingent upon the principle of exchange, not the principle of maximum individual accumulation. The difference is subtle to the insensitive human intellect, but no less vital for being so. The principle of accumulation states that I will exchange the minimum I must part with, in order to acquire the maximum I can. By contrast, the principle of exchange, founded on the acknowledgement of the systemic interdependence of our universe, recognises that we must give back, measure for measure, as much energy as we wish to take away. This is not communism, nor even socialism, for the acknowledgement that we are part of the greater must start in the individual heart. I, and I alone, can acknowledge within myself that for all value I wish to remove, I must return value. It consistently requires that I give back more than I am obliged to give. The resources of the environment, generally, and the resources of this particular Amazonian part of the system, are not free, even if they do not belong to some documented human owner. Indeed, nothing is 'free' in that sense. Whatever we take costs some part of the eco-structure something and therefore, in reality, costs us all something, for we are part of the eco-structure. Individually, we can accumulate more, consume more, until that to which we lay claim coalesces and congeals into the parody of desirability called conspicuous consumption. But at the end of our physical visit to this world, when we go back to where we originated in spirit, it is useless to us. One way or another, it returns to the system, as do our very bodies themselves.

Rainforest trees grow in the river

If, in our frenzied enthusiasm for accumulation, we temporarily change the trajectory of the resource, eventually, it still returns to the dynamic equilibrium from which we took it. Yet, perhaps, this may not be so, before the very disequilibrium we have engendered does harm to our own interests, or those of others we value within the system – our brothers and sisters and our descendants. We can flow with the system, the Tao, or we can fight it pointlessly. Either way, the Tao returns to its own dynamic equilibrium. It is inestimably bigger than we are, and it has no plans to change on account of us.

We cannot see dolphins this morning. Like all sensible creatures, they are still asleep at 6:00 am. Nor am I much more successful when it comes to piranha fishing that follows a little later. When I do catch one, and go on to eat it, fried with lime juice, on the floating house of an Amazonian Indian family, I salve my conscience with the thought that the fish, too, has killed indiscriminately in order to live. Yet, my conscience is not fooled. I still anticipate that I will fumble my way towards vegetarianism this year.

Before I leave, I am careful to give a small gift to the children of the household. It is part of putting back more than I am obliged to. And before I leave Amazonia, I must give Elcio a slightly larger gift to be used for the benefit of the locality in any way he sees fit. This, too, is an obligation that is not an obligation, if I wish to remain centred within myself and within the dynamic equilibrium of the system. As we return to the lodge, the forest is wide awake, its animal and bird inhabitants screaming at one another like deranged inmates of a wall-less Bedlam. It no longer seems angry. It has made me understand its pain. For now, both the rainforest and I are at peace.

You see, this problem that it poses, though dire, is really quite simply stated. We either learn, as a matter of principle, to put back as least as much as we take out, or the system, the Tao, eventually eliminates us as it does all disequilibrium. And in the case of the rapidly depleting rainforest, it is conceptually even more straightforward. It is my problem and it is your problem. We either solve it or we asphyxiate.

Amazon River, Brazil
January 2004

Kissing the Hand of Africa

I returned home to the UK from the rainforest in January 2004, deep in thought concerning the self-annihilation the human race seems hell-bent on imposing upon itself, through the devastation of its planet.

Though the Kyoto protocol had been adopted in 1997, its first commitment period did not come into force until 2008. It was to be some years before a more general awareness of consequences of our ecological delinquency permeated into mass consciousness. By 2016, Thomas Lovejoy's editorial in the journal 'Scientific Advances' had concluded that deforestation in the Amazon was about to reach a threshold beyond which the region's tropical rainforest might undergo irreversible changes that transform the landscape into degraded savannah with sparse, shrubby plant cover and low biodiversity. At the time of writing, two years later in 2018, nothing has happened that suggests a change in our march to asphyxiation.

For the rest of 2004, the practicalities of my own normal life continued: managing my rapid hearing loss, earning a living as proprietor of a business and moving house to a new home in the New Forest. But perhaps the single most important personal event that took place that year was the explosive appearance of a small furry animal in my life. Matt, my hearing dog, had arrived. That first year we spent learning to live and work in partnership together is documented in my book, If It Wasn't For That Dog.

By the end of the year, I knew it was time for me to travel again. Matt went to stay with friends, while I flew to South Africa. I

31

wanted to experience first-hand the capability we carry within ourselves to make genuine, lasting change. I was also to discover the extraordinary power of forgiveness. The visit to the Amazon rainforest had been for learning. But forgiveness? Forgiveness is different. Forgiveness is about loving. And discovering more about loving was the next step on my journey.

Days 1–2: Johannesburg to Kruger

It's a cool morning here in Cape Town and I'm sitting outside on the patio of the President Hotel (opened by Nelson Mandela in 1998, according to the plaque on the wall), looking over the sea, while the fountain plays over the pool. A few hopeful hotel guests sit at tables or on loungers waiting for the sun to decide if it is going to take off its cloudy shroud and go for full frontal for the day. If it does, I'll likely move into the bar to write, not being a great lover of direct sunlight. That has been one of the issues I have needed to manage on this voyage. Temperatures have risen as high as 47° (and yes, that's centigrade – 116° Fahrenheit, in old money) in the north of the country, making me thankful for our fully insulated, air-conditioned coach.

As we ate up the miles from Jo'burg to the Kruger National Park, I had dozed a little to compensate for the lack of sleep on the overnight flight from London. But we are only two hours ahead of UK time here, so there's no jet lag and the effects of the flight soon passed. When I awoke, I contented myself with drinking down as many of the various images of a new country as 100 km per hour will permit, and listening to such parts of the tour guide's commentary as I could hear.

Linda, our guide, is a thin, white, South African woman, about 5' 5" tall and seemingly in her mid-forties. A gaunt and heavily made-up face seems to segregate her public presentation from her inner self. I am unable to touch her on the non-physical level. Actually, I doubt she allows anyone to touch her, though I have no insight as to why. So, I simply listen to the sound of her voice as it wafts down the speaker system from the front of the coach. We pass a power station on our right: "South Africa," she says, "has a wonderful infrastructure. The old Government spent all its money on the infrastructure. So, we have for Africa, wonderful roads and cheap power. But nothing was spent on the people. Now, the new Government spends money on the people, and that is good." The tension in her voice and the slightly stilted presentation sound less than wholly convincing. I am reminded of the guides that would show western tourists around the former Soviet bloc countries before the Berlin Wall came down, anxious to impress visitors with the approved doctrine, yet failing to hold an inner conviction as to its veracity. "BMW," she continues, "assembles cars here because of the cheap power. Not because of cheap labour anymore, because now, we have the minimum wage and that is good. But because our power production is so good and so cheap, it costs them one-tenth to assemble cars here of what it would cost in Germany. And we need to attract many more companies like them, for our biggest economic problem is unemployment." My attention drifts back to the road flashing past our vehicle, the vast empty green space, the first building blocks of my understanding of this huge country.

As the miles pass, and we approach the Panorama district and Mpumalanga, on the edge of which the Kruger National Park lies, I am aware of something a little unusual happening outside. In each little hamlet we pass, I see the haphazard wooden shacks that used to characterise so many newscasts coming out of the South Africa in the 1980s and early 90s, before the demise of apartheid. But now, they are interspersed with new buildings – breezeblock houses of substance and stability. Some are untidy, quickly and haphazardly erected, their construction still undermined by the mental constraints of habitual poverty. But there are also others, built perhaps more recently, with care and attention paid to arched doorways, eye-catching layouts and quality brick facades. As the old limiting beliefs begin to fade, new possibilities have occurred to the homemakers.

Mpumalanga, towards Kruger

The intercom crackles and Linda's voice breaks in again. "Notice the housing," she says. "The people can ask the government for loans to build houses, and everywhere the state of accommodation is improving." There's that phrase again, 'the people'. Is Linda one of 'the people' now, I wonder? In a country ruled by a black majority, does a white middle-class woman count as 'the people'? And where do I, a traveller from a foreign land, fit in? Am I 'the people' because my home country took in so many refugees and stood, sometimes, against apartheid? Or am I not 'the people' because my pale skin makes me stand out like a white whale grazing on the plankton of tourist attractions in a sea of black humanity? Of course, what I'm really asking, and what more than everything else I'm here to find out is, 'Where is the heart of the New South Africa?' some fifteen years after the demolition of darkness that was the end of apartheid. It is only day two. It is too soon to tell.

Day 3:   Kruger National Park

I have been a true tourist in South Africa for a couple of days now, and the fantasy world in which all tourists live is troublesome to me. I know, of course, that we are being presented with the best that the country has to offer its valued visitors, and I justify my enjoyment of this luxury, inaccessible to local inhabitants, in my knowledge that I bring both foreign exchange and employment to its people. But my economic superiority affords me power, power to negotiate or twist arms in my buying power, to withhold my wealth or bestow it where I chose. I know that if one is not careful, such power causes cataracts to grow over the eyes of the heart. The only way I know of avoiding this is to give when it is not expected, pay more than is required and offer warmth and smiles instead of the rigidity and exclusion that my status permits.

We were up at 5:00 am this morning to drive through Kruger in an open-sided 4x4. The hotel packed each of us off with ample breakfast in a plastic box and we left for the park before 6:00 am. Two hours of early morning drive though the bush, over roads paved and unpaved, afforded us the long-anticipated sightings of elephants and hippos, zebras and giraffes, wildebeest and buffalo, not to mention innumerable encounters with the lesser-spotted albino tourists.

Uninvited breakfast guest at Kruger

After two hours of bouncing over potholes and ruts, we pulled into a well-maintained camping area for breakfast.

I buy a coffee and settle down for half an hour's blessed immobility in the as yet, gentle early morning sun. But the hotel has over-provided on the breakfast. So, I pick a hard-boiled egg, yoghurt and a banana in preference to sandwiches, apples, biscuits and the other delicacies, and leave the rest aside with no further thought, for I have had enough. I contemplate the beauty of the scenery, the warmth of the African day, my fortune in being able to be here. And when it is time to go, I discard the remains of my breakfast in the bin provided, careful not to impose my refuse on this continent. But as I walk away, now comes my first impromptu confrontation with the real South Africa. For something (a sound? a feeling? my guilt?) makes me turn and I see that a middle-aged black woman has opened the bin behind me and is extracting my picnic box and those of several other tourists. She stands closely over the bin, dressed in bright-coloured shawl and skirt, and not obviously hungry. She studies carefully, her experienced hands hovering over the boxes ready to extract whatever viable nutrition she can find to help feed her family. Everything I have discarded is taken, and secreted away in her plastic carrier bag for tonight's dinner. She hesitates over a half-eaten cake in someone else's box, turning it this way and that, exactly as if she were evaluating a mango on a market stall. The cake is deemed acceptable, and it, too, is consigned to the security of her carrier bag. My eyes close and I sink back in shame; for my sister and I, the currency of half-eaten cake holds wholly different values. She turns to leave, triumphant that her morning's hunt amongst the albino tourists has yielded food for her family. Both shaken and stirred, I turn and head for the 4x4. 'Blessed are the poor,' I find myself thinking, 'for theirs is the kingdom of heaven.' She is poor and hers is the kingdom of heaven. But, in my wealth, it is I who am poverty stricken.

'Border Post' means something different here

It is time to leave Kruger and make the short coach trip to Swaziland, where our destination for New Year's Eve is the hotel of Pig's Peak. We are four days into our tour now, and amongst my companions, the barriers of unfamiliarity are beginning to lower a little, giving way to the early stages of a group identity. From my old management consultancy

days, the phases of group dynamics come to mind –
'forming, norming, storming, reforming', if I have it
correctly, from memory. We are some twenty in number,
and all but one are Brits, varying in age from about thirty
to sixty years and all single, for as many reasons as there
are to be single. Some, I learn, are like me, divorced. Some
are in the early stages of widow or widower-hood. And
then, there's me – alone, in part, because against all odds
I have learned to value the intimacy of self-awareness that
comes more easily from aloneness.

'Embracing my aloneness, I find connections
everywhere.

Turning to face my fears, I find the warrior,
who dwells within,'

as Jennifer Wellwood, the Californian psychologist, has
it in her poem. As the group begins to gel, I feel
simultaneously embraced, by the various small gestures of
friendship my companions offer (a touch on the arm, a
check to ensure that I have heard an announcement), and
repelled, due both to my deafness that excludes me from
the ability to conduct small talk across a dinner table and
to my impatience with superficiality. For, in truth, I prefer
to touch people more meaningfully, heart to heart, deep
talking unto deep. In practice, many people find depth
threatening. There is an opening, an exposing of one's
emotional soft underbelly in permitting another to enter
one's deep places – and that can be scary. We are

frightened of what others might do if we give them opportunity and ammunition. Though it is true that we are fulfilled in deep connection, it is also in accessing our depths that others can cause us pain. I have learned to accept depth as the opportunity arises, going as far as another person will permit and showing no resentment when the cage door swings shut and the sign reads 'no entry'. Someone who closes the door to psychic or spiritual connection has learned from life's experience to do so when they sense danger, and the exposure of their own weakness. I want only to be a catalyst for love, and for light, for joy and for learning. So, I do not rattle on the bars to get in. The lion will emerge when it is time to roar.

The coach groans and grinds slowly up the steep mountain trail to the hotel at Pig's Peak. We go through the usual motions of checking in, to a welcome of local fruit juice and porters who carry our cases up to our rooms. We are each less than thrilled to find that over this holiday season, the air conditioning has broken down throughout the hotel and will not be fixed during our one-night stay. But tonight, we will see in the New Year outdoors, eating at long trestle tables by the pool and illuminating our way into 2005 by candlelight and fireworks. We are high up in the mountains, looking down over a lush green valley laid out below. It is cool enough. For the coming few hours of sleep, I will not miss the air conditioning too much.

This evening, I do something I have not generally been prone to doing. I'm determined I will see in the New Year with this group of new friends. I will embrace the light-heartedness and gaiety that I normally exclude, for the span of one evening. In the process of doing so, I can't help feeling that I am not the only one on this trip who is not normally drawn to the superficial. There will be those that prefer depth but who do tolerate chaff as a precursor to connecting with others. And there will be others still, who live from the premise that the only safe way to connect is superficially. At this stage, I have no way of knowing who, in this respect, is who.

So it is that I find myself sitting on the end of a long table, unable to ask for the lights to be turned up or the music to be turned down (assertive behaviour such as this, I have just learned in lip reading classes) and I wait for events to unfold. I look around with no particular agenda, at least, that is, until the tumblers drop into place and the door swings open. For opposite me sits Heather, a polite and pretty woman of about forty. She's attractive, and I've sought to open a conversation with her on more than one occasion (well what do you expect, I'm a normal healthy single man, you know!). Like all the ladies in our party, she is made up and dressed up, and exhibits all the communication signals that she is enjoying herself. But a shadow crosses my mental movie screen and momentarily, another picture passes through my mind. I see a metaphor – the most beautiful of sailing ships, sails billowing in the breeze, figurehead newly painted and decks freshly swabbed, ploughing her way through fair seas. Yet, I also see how dangerously low the ship sits in the water. The question arises in my mind, 'I wonder what lies beneath the waterline that causes her to ride so low?' In a moment, the picture is gone, and the more immediate reality of the

New Year's evening – and in particular, Heather sitting opposite me – returns. She has shown no inclination to talk to me beyond the most superficial of polite conversations. Yet, I am curious now to know what lies beneath Heather's spiritual waterline. I sit quietly for a few minutes, not trying to resist as the lines of a poem appear in my mind. It is the last day of 2004 and this is only the second poem that has come to me all year. The Poet within me has been silent a long time, and I'm delighted to find he is back. But he will not linger if I do not honour him. So, I scoot off to my room for pen and paper. Returning to my seat and the environment that sired the poem, I write the concepts that I am seeing in whatever words come to mind. I can polish cadence and alliteration in the days that follow, if I choose. But the heart of the poem is in the metaphor. I lay my sacrifice on the altar before The Poet and wait for his flames to consume it. If he is satisfied with the offering, tomorrow and the next day, there will be a poem. But tonight is New Year and I find myself, much to my surprise, dancing enticingly towards 2005 with the very pretty young temporary tour guide who is chaperoning us through Swaziland. Just as I am thinking that I shall be dancing across midnight, my pattern is broken by the incongruity of a Scottish Piper in kilt and full regalia. He has appeared in order to pipe us into the New Year. In the old tradition, I find myself with strangers in a strange land and sing 'Auld Lang Syne'.

Day 5:   Swaziland

Our schedule for the first day of the New Year is to drive down through Swaziland and its capital Manzini, then back over the border and down to Durban for a short flight to Port Elizabeth. As we make our way back down the mountain through the early morning mists, Linda's voice crackles over the coach's intercom once again. She talks of the King of Swaziland and the country's constitutional ritual for his appointment. We are in a land where men traditionally take many wives. And, of course, in order to stand out as a figurehead, the king must have the largest number of wives. Accordingly, Linda tells us, the last king had about 100 wives and around 200 children. Upon his death, she says, each king's successor is chosen by an age-old method. First, the focus is upon the mother of the future king. From amongst the many wives, only those with a single child – a boy – are eligible to be considered. Then, the number is further reduced by considering only those of blameless character. Anyone who has had ill spoken of them by anybody is excluded. From this (presumably rather smaller) number, the son is chosen who will succeed the deceased king. This time round, we are told, the chosen prince was having rather a good time studying in London and was none too keen to return. But he eventually allowed himself to be persuaded and is widely regarded as doing a pretty good job. He is also making headway in providing for his own succession, for at twenty-six years of age, he already has eighteen wives. I muse briefly on the fact that, personally, I have been unable to keep one wife happy, so, what would I have made of eighteen of them? Hmm... better not go there. Well, I guess, if you're going to run an absolute monarchy, it's as good a way as any for ensuring succession to the royal lineage.

We make our way down to Manzini, where we stop at a craft market – a series of makeshift huts at the side of the road. Out of the coach we tumble, clutching our 200 rand notes, passports to retail paradise. Each stall sports similar goods – an unending Noah's ark procession of carved wooden animals in all shapes and sizes, masks, chairs, beads and bangles, local woven goods. I stop to look at some scarves that I might take back for my daughters. As I show interest, the young proprietor of the stall approaches and mentions a price – a rather high one. I pull back a little, but she has positioned herself between me and the entrance to the shop. I have the option either of pushing past and so behaving rudely in a foreign country, or continuing further back into the shop to evaluate more of her stock. Naturally, I choose the latter. But the further back I go, the closer she approaches, stepping now well into my aura space, seeking, I believe, a sacral chakra sexual response. I look at her more closely now. She can't be more than sixteen or so, but clearly has learned something already about how to sell to different categories of potential buyers. I presumably fall into the category of 'middle-aged men, travelling alone and therefore, suitable to being influenced by sexuality.' Now, she brushes up against me, making sure her breast presses briefly against my arm and her leg against my hand. Then, fortuitously for me, she unconsciously breaks state by pushing a finger up her nose! Perhaps it's normal social behaviour in Swaziland. I don't know and I don't want to. I take the opportunity of the shift in energy to move back towards the front of the shop. She follows of course. We agree a price for two of the scarves, which turn out to be more of tablecloth proportion. I hand over a note and walk away with a smile, my gifts for my daughters in my hands. It is at that moment I notice a much older women sitting outside the front of the shop, who has been observing clearly all that has transpired. An image flashes into my mind of a lioness watching a cub play with its prey. My economic muscle has been nothing but soft underbelly tissue in the paws of the lionesses.

I stop for another purchase – a large wooden hippo (instantly christened Henry) who will make a rather fine doorstop in my little cob cottage back in the New Forest. With ego somewhat bruised from my last encounter, I find myself negotiating harder than I would normally chose to do in such circumstances. But I am still licking the wound inflicted by the lion cub, and have a need to demonstrate that I am still a force to be reckoned with in the African bush. Henry and I make our way back to the coach, where he becomes the subject of considerable mirth. As the following days pass, more and more of my companions start asking to see him. I tell them he is under sedation lest the transition from his homeland to a foreign country prove too stressful to him, or that he is resting in our room, studying an English primer in preparation for arrival in his new home. Some of my companions giggle at this. Others seem to think I am being serious and regard me as an even stranger individual than they had previously thought. Either way, the truth about my oddness is now definitively out.

Day 10:   To Cape Town

The days have slipped past as easily as oysters on the tongue. We made our way down through Swaziland to the Ithala Game Reserve and continued the next day down the N2 coastal road to Durban. I have admired the land management in this vast country, with mile upon mile of timber cultivation indicating a sophisticated and well-managed economy. Yet, as the coach reverberates rhythmically through yet more miles, we pass more of the tiny wooden shacks and the empty bush land that reminds you that South Africa is an irreconcilable mix of First and Third World economies. Durban and Port Elizabeth on the Indian Ocean coast bring no relief from this see-saw perception, throwing us back into the vibrancy of a modern sophisticated economy. We pass into the South Africans' playground of the Tsitsikamma, Plettenberg Bay and Knysna, where the property prices are measured in millions of rand. Then comes our final long day in the coach, to cover the last few hundred kilometres to Cape Town. Arriving in the city, we make straight for Table Mountain. On this perfect summer's afternoon the wind is non-existent, the cable cars are running, the queues are minimal and the view is astounding. It is unquestionably the finest cable car view I have ever seen, and I would have no trouble believing it is the best in the world. However, the time for play is over, for tomorrow we have been offered the opportunity to take what is somewhat euphemistically called a cultural tour – more aptly described as a look back into apartheid and an exploration of what life is like for the largely unemployed mass of people in the townships. It is for this that I have come.

Day 11:   District Six and the Townships

For the morning's 'cultural tour', we have an 8:30 am start. Out of the twenty or so of us on the tour, just nine chose to take this trip. I can only guess as to why the rest of the party are visiting this country but I'm thinking their reasons have more to do with experiencing the opulence that South Africa can offer the few, rather than the challenges that are the experiences of the many.

Our guide for the day is a mixed-race man in his thirties, called Hassan. He and I have spent half an hour chatting before departure. I had struggled against deafness to maintain a conversation with him for much longer than I would normally be willing. I do this because of what he represents to me. I know that through him and because of him, today, I will touch the real South Africa.

The guidebooks do nothing to prepare you for the reality of the experience. The museum is housed in an old chapel building in what was indeed known as District Six. We have driven perhaps fifteen minutes from our hotel and alight from the coach in a quiet and unassuming part of Cape Town. At the entrance of the museum is a plaque. It reads:

All Who Pass By;
Remember with Shame
the many thousands of people
who lived for generations
in District Six and other part of the city,
and were forced by law to leave their homes
because of the colour of their skins....
Father Forgive Us.

I enter the building from the day that is already bright, wholly unprepared for the darkness and light that both await me within.

The museum's ground floor is essentially a single large open space. Its first floor is a mezzanine gallery, where the old church's overspill congregation would have sat, back in the consecrated days. As we step inside the door, I turn first to my right, where a series of revolving boards tell the story of District Six. It is essentially the history of apartheid. The process of removal and marginalisation began in the early twentieth century. But it was in 1966 that the District was designated 'Whites Only', by a parliamentary motion sealed with a Prime Minister's pen. By 1982 it had been enshrined by the bulldozer and the identification card into the destruction of the homes of some sixty thousand people. They were removed to the area of Cape Flats, to occupy what subsequently became known as townships.

On the floor at District Six Museum

My group calls me to the front so that I can hear the words of our guide, Noor Ibrahim, who begins my enlightenment as to the nature of the New South Africa. For Noor, an elderly Muslim, explains in simple, quiet tones, a gentle smile held permanently on his face, the story of his life as a resident of District Six: how his home was destroyed, his family forced out of the spaces where they had long since sunk their roots. He points to the floor of the chapel-museum where almost all of the space is devoted to an enormous, colourful map of District Six. The authorities had razed the buildings and erased the roads from the face of the earth, but they were incapable of removing the memories stored in the minds of its people. He points out the location of his former house and I see that many, many others have also written their names in the spaces where their own homes had stood. Noor leads us into a small room, made up as a typical District Six home would have looked before the coming of the bulldozers. It is nothing special – just a couple of beds, a small table and chairs and a cooking area. The shelving is decorated with artistically cut newspaper. These are a people who can see beauty wherever they look.

And now, the spirit of the museum begins to descend upon me, as Noor has seen it do on visitors countless times before. He opens the door of the little mocked-up room to allow us to wander around. I step back into the main museum area and ask him how he deals with the anger he must feel. "There is no anger now," he says quietly, a smile on his face. "I have forgiven, and seek only reconciliation." And that is so clearly the energy of this edifice to a humbling and shameful past. These people have learned something of inestimable importance: that returning hate and anger to hate and anger merely breeds yet more hate and anger. But to return gentleness to hatred, forgiveness to anger and reconciliation to intransigence, conceives love. And when gestated for as long as is needful, love gives birth to growth, and to joy, and to peace. These are the qualities I see on the face of Noor and in every exhibit in the museum as I make my way slowly and reverently round the room. The floor is inscribed with poetry from the age of incarceration. Those who command imprisonment can take away distractions and withhold the music of song, but they cannot silence the eloquence of the spoken word, nor can they disfigure the beauty of cadence and rhyme. This, it seems to me, is why we turn to poetry when all else fails us. I visit the bookshop before I leave the museum. I buy a copy of Noor's life story which he signs for me, together with two books of formerly banned poetry that dates from the days of darkness. As I prepare to leave, I am transfixed by a large plaque by the door, which reads as in the following image.

The District Six Museum: a final message

Shaking, I step back down into the morning sunlight and make for the coach, in the knowledge that I have stood in the presence of a gatekeeper of God, in the entrance hall of heaven. The words echo through the cavern of my mind: 'Father, forgive us, for we knew not what they did.'

Climbing back up into the coach, it is clear that the museum has a similar impact on my fellow travellers, for there are tears in many eyes. A quiet contemplative energy has replaced the normal happy-go-lucky holiday atmosphere. Hassan, too, is quiet now, as he takes the microphone. He speaks of his own anger that was: the anger of a man classified as coloured and excluded, alienated for the utterly illogical reason of the tint of his skin. And of course, once you start exploring this corridor of thought, it takes you through doors that simply lead to more questions; questions as to why we segregate and separate ourselves from anyone; why, for the sake of ego, we have to think of ourselves as higher than anyone, or for that matter, lower than anyone. Throughout this journey, I have been reading Wayne Dyer's book, *The Power of Intention*. He makes the point that if we once stop thinking of ourselves as our bodies and refer to the energy of intention (for me, the Tao), then, we can let go of all segregation of ourselves from other men and women, acknowledging that we are all one, all the same joined in the Source of the Energy. Hassan doesn't use these terms though. As we make our way out to Cape Flats and the townships, he speaks simply and softly of how he felt on hearing Nelson Mandela's speech when first freed from captivity. How, after twenty-seven years of detention on

Robben Island, Mandela was able to talk immediately of forgiveness and reconciliation. As Hassan had listened to him, he had thought to himself, "If that man can talk of forgiveness after twenty-seven years of incarceration at the hands of evil, I too, can forgive the much smaller ills done to me." As the coach rumbles through Cape Town, I find myself wondering what might have happened in South Africa if Nelson Mandela had been not a forgiving man of reconciliation, but a vindictive man of retribution. I am done now, lost in thought.

Mid-morning brings us to the Cape Flats Township. We are instructed to leave valuables on the coach, which will meet us later. But it's ok to take cameras and to take pictures, so long as we first ask permission of anyone we wish to photograph. So, we step down into the sun once more and are introduced to our township guide, Gladstone. I'm told we will be physically safe and I believe what I'm told. However, I have doubts as to my emotional safety. Hassan asks Gladstone the meaning of his name. He says, it means a happy stone. I think it superfluous to point out to these gentlemen the details of nineteenth-century English history, if they don't already know! Gladstone is a slightly diminutive, well-spoken and obviously intelligent young black man of perhaps eighteen or so. He commences our tour with a visit to a small project centre in the township, which is working on recycling and ecology, together with local artwork. From here, he leads us on a walking tour into the township proper.

We start in what Gladstone refers to as the 'working class' district. I presume the term to have the same meaning as it does at home, and wonder if there is a middle class district and an upper class district. I am oblivious at this stage to the fact that the term 'working class' distinguishes the part of the township in which people have work from the part where unemployment is near universal. Here, to be referred to as working class is to be esteemed. As we look around the dusty but well-kept streets, we see houses in pristine condition, carefully pointed brick walls, neat garden fences. Perhaps it's not so bad to live in the township after all. But as we approach the end of the road, Gladstone tells us that we are about to enter the hostel district. I cast a glance across the road and see a series of large buildings, many run down to the point of dereliction. "These buildings," Gladstone tells us, "were originally built for the male migrant workers who came to work in Cape Town. Here, they were permitted to live in hostels, six to a room, sending money back to their families as they could." Now, the hostels are slowly being converted into flats. But until such time as each building is converted, it is occupied by several families. "We are going to go into a hostel," Gladstone tells us. "You may take pictures and ask questions of the people you meet." We look at one another and swallow hard in anticipation of the sights that will shortly be offered to our delicate first-world eyes. Then, we are across the road, into the dusty area between the hostel buildings that is littered with refuse and burned-out cars, the flotsam of life in the townships. Here, a pole supports a makeshift washing line strung between two posts, the washing hung so as to avoid its fouling on the rusty blue van with no headlights – a vehicle stripped of all saleable or reusable parts. Next to it stand two rusting oil drums. A pile of rubble, bricks and sticks, lies neglected in the middle of the open area between the buildings where the children play.

Yes, it is inhabited

We pick our way carefully around the car and discarded piles of useless rubbish towards the outside staircase that leads up to the dormitory designated for our visit. We make our way up, crocodile style, grateful for the false sense of security that comes from a group numbering only nine wealthy 'haves' amongst this overwhelming number of 'have-nots'. We enter a central 'living room', maybe twenty feet by ten, furnished with built-in table and benches. Once, the bare brick walls had been painted yellow. Now, they are faded and peeling, stained with who knows how many years of human occupation by who knows how many generations, each too aware of their 'have not' status to display any sense of ownership that might otherwise have given this tired-out, stressed-out building some emotional investment. The floor is a mass of broken lino tiles. The ceiling is blackened by years of soot from cooking and heating. Off the main living room are several bedrooms, some padlocked. I can see through the crack that, mercifully, they are a little better furnished and better cared for. The smell is bearable in all rooms but the one that serves as a toilet, where an open urinal uncompromisingly announces its presence in time-honoured fashion. I confess I am relieved when Gladstone leads us back down the outside staircase into the sunshine.

As we continue our walk, I find myself assessing how I am feeling and considering how I should be feeling. Am I a voyeur, dipping into the low places where humanity hides its offcasts, so that I can feign some kind of affected care and knowledge when asked what I did in South Africa? Am I helping by bringing currency and awareness to this place of more need than I have ever seen before in my life? At this point, I truly cannot say. But I am reminded of a sci-fi movie I saw once, the title long since vanished from my memory, where visitors from the future step back into famous disasters of the twentieth century to experience a more exciting reality than their own. I remember them being shepherded crocodile fashion by a tour guide through the smoke and the fires of the San Francisco earthquake of 1904, fully present, yet fully isolated from the effects. Here, we first-worlders are stepping back in time, for these are the conditions that might well have been common in nineteenth-century London.

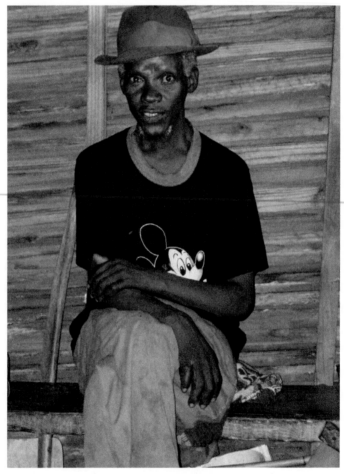

In the pub

But it's not over till it's over and it's going to become more challenging yet. Now, Gladstone leads us down between the dormitory buildings between more burnt-out vehicles and piles of disfigured waste into the midst of a small group of makeshift shanty shacks. I look down as I walk, my eyes drawn to a scraggy dog licking an open sore on its leg. I shudder and think of Matt, safe at home, well fed and well looked after by a host family in my absence. Then, we stop. We are standing in the glare of the mid-morning sun outside the open door of a wooden shack. We look at one another, anticipating that we are about to be invited inside.

I am relieved – and I think everyone else is too – that it does not turn out to be a primitive home, but instead is a combination of brewery and pub. This is where the local beer is brewed and sold in small buckets that look as though they hold about two litres. We sit down on benches that run down one side of the little building and I take a few moments to acclimatise to my environment. The shack is a similar size to the shanty homes we have passed so many times on this trip. It may well have served as somebody's home at some time past. It's about twenty feet by fifteen, almost windowless, with a dirt floor. The walls are made of whatever came to hand at the time of building – wooden planks, bits of fibreboard, bits of what looks like asbestos – anything that will keep out the weather, however temporarily. Outside, the roof is covered with black plastic sheets, weighed down by several large bags of sand to hold them in place when the winds come. Inside, a couple of lightweight timbers stretch across the ceiling, about eight feet high, acting as supporting joists. At some time, one of them has been broken in a couple of places. But no matter, the break has easily been remedied by timber props – just be careful not to bump against them inadvertently and thereby, bring the whole structure crashing down on top of you.

Again, the prevailing smell is of soot and tobacco smoke but this time, it has a beery, alcoholic kind of overtone to it. Ironically, now, of all times, comes to mind the phrase, 'Be it ever so humble, there's no place like home'.

Gladstone explains in his incongruously educated accent that we are here to sample the local beer. My usual response when offered beer is to say that I never drink it and that I've drunk wine all my adult life. Somehow, I don't think that's going to be quite appropriate here. The lady brewer passes a bucket of beer to Gladstone. He demonstrates how to drink it, blowing off the froth, putting it to his lips before passing it to the first of our group who is encouraged to do the same. And now, the can is passed from person to person, as if it were a peace pipe around the campfire in an Indian tepee village in a western movie. Many cannot stomach the thought of putting it to their lips and simply pass it on. My turn comes. It seems to me that to refuse this offer is to refuse Africa and her hospitality, however distasteful beer is to me, and whatever the risk that partaking might carry. I lift the can to my lips, blow off the froth and drink. It is warm beer, no more, no less. My right of passage is over and I am free to emerge into the sunlight, somehow feeling more accepted by this community than before. Perhaps, the reality is that in the simple generosity of these people, I was already accepted. Once again, the change has not been in others or in my environment. It has been in me.

Improvements are ongoing

The crocodile now weaves its way out of the shanty area and back between the dormitory buildings. This time, I notice that on one side of the road, the buildings have been converted into attractive blocks of flats. These are freshly painted and neatly maintained, each entrance proudly sporting a street number, and yes, I would be content to live in such accommodation myself. Across the road stand the – as yet – unconverted blocks. But where we are now, I notice the concrete pillars that have been sunken into the ground between them to support the exterior walls that are about to be built, wrapping around the existing building like cloaks, completing and extending them for acceptable habitation in a modern twenty-first-century society.

But much remains to be done

We are easing our way away from the dormitory building now and I begin to breathe more easily. Then, I sense motion behind me – footsteps running. Before I have time to turn or to make meaning of this, a small hand slips into mine and I hear a little voice hopefully say, "Picture?" Now, I turn and look down. She can't be more than three, very dark skinned, completely bald, and dressed in red from head to toe. Her eyes shine and her face beams love and friendliness into mine. Inevitably, my own face breaks into a smile, and with no more common words between us than 'Picture', I pass her hand to one of my companions, Kate, a medical doctor, aged about forty. Kate poses with her while I take their picture together. I take Kate's camera and repeat the process. For each picture, our newfound friend beams directly into the camera. When the joyful interlude is over, she scampers off happily to play. I cannot tell you how relieved I am to see this ray of sunshine shining out from the abject poverty I have just witnessed. These children, and so many others like her, are able to make happiness and hope the cornerstone of their future on the true face of the new South Africa.

So now, the crocodile makes its way into the sunshine and there is but one more ordeal left for us. As we approach the meeting point for the coach, we stand across the road from the large mass of the township that is a true shanty town. Gladstone does not attempt to take us in here. He knows we have already seen everything our feeble first-world eyes can accommodate. Instead, he gives us his farewell speech. "Thank you," he says, "for your courage in coming to visit us today, for seeing the new South Africa in all she has achieved and all the challenges she is still grappling with."

'This man wants to thank us?' I ask myself, amazed. As I approach the coach, I take his hands in mine. "I can't begin to thank you for what you've shown me today," I tell him. "I needed to know and to understand how it is for you and your people. To the best of my ability, I will act on what I see."

"Thank you," Gladstone replies, "I'll take that as a compliment."

"Oh," I say, feeling overwhelmed. "You have no idea how much of a compliment it is." I shake both of his hands simultaneously. With relief, I climb the stairs back, up into my safe, air-conditioned life.

That night, I sleep fitfully. I awaken repeatedly to the lingering visions of the township. At one point, I find myself wondering what it might cost to pay for paint to paint all the hostels, inside and out. Then, I realise the pointlessness of the gesture, given that the hostels will soon be renovated anyway. The next day, the nine of us that went on the trip debate what we have seen. I offer the opinion that if we return in ten years, perhaps, the shanty town will be gone, replaced by neat, habitable buildings. "No," counters another in our group, "for as fast as these people are housed, more will come from the countryside, in search of employment." And I have to acknowledge the superiority of her argument, for it was always thus, in a low employment, agrarian society transitioning into industrialisation. And all this, of course, deals with only one of South Africa's problems – the poverty that arises from unemployment. I have not even begun to address my thinking to the consequence of Aids or a dozen other worries that South Africa, and all of Africa, faces. Yet, despite the depths of depravation that I have witnessed today, it is my firm and enduring belief that the new South Africa will rise and rise and rise. For it is founded on forgiveness, and is being built with bricks of love, bonded with the mortar of enduring commitment.

Day 13: Umhlanga

Three days have passed since our confrontation with South Africa's 'challenges', as Gladstone phrased it. This is time enough to allow the realisation to flow in at both the physical and the energy level. I am not alone in the profound disturbance I have experienced and the sense of practical helplessness it imposes. Conversations with others in the group have revealed the deep cuts that the knives of deprivation awareness have inflicted. We are all experiencing the simultaneous flows of desire to help and of helplessness initiated by the visit. One person has passed comment that she felt like telling Dulux about the hostels and asking than to take on their repainting as a project. Another tells me that the side of poverty we have seen, though arresting, does not compare with what she has seen in India, which she describes as the worst culture shock she has ever experienced. We are all deeply affected. Who could see what we have seen and not be touched?

But tours are transient and ours has moved on. We are spending a couple of quiet days at a beach resort just outside Durban before returning home. At breakfast, we hear of a flea market a few miles away, and four of us decide to take a taxi to visit it. I have a few final presents I want to buy before we fly away home. It is Sunday morning, the sun is shining and the crowds are milling around the stalls on the edge of the Indian Ocean. Stallholders call my attention to carvings, clothing, sunglasses, and a host of other gaily coloured eye-catching delights. Before I get very far though, I see an elderly coloured woman sitting on a bench holding a sign. 'I need money for food', it reads, 'not drink. I never drink alcohol.' I slow down, hesitate. The issue is not new to me, and I know the only action I can take that satisfies my soul. I slip my hand into my pocket and pass her all the coins I find; just a few pennies to me, perhaps, a meal to her.

But my Guides are not satisfied with this small sacrifice, for there are many, many more beggars in the market this morning. So, I let my intuition take over and to some, but not all, I give small sums. Am I right to exclude any in such an apparently arbitrary manner? I will never know the circumstances of any one of these people. All I have to rely on are my conscience and my intuition.

We walk around the stalls, pausing here to look at a man squeezing drinks from sugar cane, stopping there for the ladies in our small party to try on a blouse or a belt. The music is booming out of a speaker somewhere high above my head; the crowd is pressing and panting, pressing and panting, like waves surging back and forth on the beach. Then, quite suddenly, I find myself separated from my party, and standing without pre-intent beside a beggar sitting on a grassy corner. He is mixed race, a thin, gaunt man in his thirties, with a short stubby beard. He moves his head, seeking to catch the eye of those passing by. When he does, he holds out his hand for whatever he can attract. You would be tempted to wonder what such an individual is doing, begging in a Sunday morning flea market, if it wasn't for the wheelchair behind him; that and the callipers he wears on his emaciated, useless legs that are stretched out in front of him, almost at right angles to one another.

There is no decision to make, other than the amount I must give. I pass him a note. He nods his thanks to me and averts his eyes, a reaction developed, I assume, in response to the many occasions on which people passing here have given him gifts and sought to move on swiftly, perhaps, in response to the emotion that eye contact with one such as this raises in us. But our transaction is not yet complete. I lean forward and take his hand tightly in mine for a moment. This man is Africa, and I have a deep-felt need to touch Africa. He looks into my eyes and speaks rapidly, in what language I cannot tell, for the noise around me is too loud for me to hear. Yet, I hear his words unmistakably in my spirit, and the words need no translation. "Thank you, thank you so much, you understand. You understand." Without warning, in the language of the deeps, he draws my hand to his face and presses it to his lips. I am shaken, honoured by the gesture. Gently, I bend further forward, raise his hand to my own face and touch it to my lips. "Namaste," I whisper. "I honour in you that which is eternal."

And as I write this in the café of the Beverly Hill hotel looking out over a drab grey sea, having first completed a filling lunch I didn't really need, I am but a fifteen-minute drive, and yet, a whole world away from him.

Today, I have kissed the hand of Africa. I have yet to touch her soul.

Umhlanga, South Africa
January 2005

In Search of Namaste

I returned from Africa deepened and challenged. Yet, the reality is that I live in the very different circumstances of a first-world country and economy, and it was not long before my life needed to return to normal. I worked at my job, I wrote my books, and I adjusted to continuing hearing loss and living with my hearing dog. Much of this is documented in If It Wasn't For That Dog.

The years slipped by, until, in 2015, I withdrew from the formal workplace to concentrate full time on writing. In 2016, my old friend Rj, a sound healer (www.sweepingsounds.com), came to visit me after some years without meeting. In the way it can be in a true, deep, friendship, we simply recommenced where we had left off. Rj lives in Thailand. During the conversation, he told me that later that year, he would be travelling to Nepal to undertake advanced training and buy more singing bowls. Instantly, I knew I would be going with him.

But there was something else I needed to do first. Having, by this time, reached a state of near profound deafness, I was scheduled to receive a cochlear implant. A processor on the outside of my head would 'hear', and transmit electronic sound to a surgically inserted array of electrodes implanted onto my cochlear. This would send the signal directly up my auditory nerve to my brain, replacing the inactive hair cells on my cochlear, which, in hearing people, transmit sound signals. With an operation to be undertaken at the end of July to insert the device in my head, I would face silence for a month, whilst waiting for the wound to heal, before the external part of the machine could be fitted. The visible external part of the device would be attached at the beginning of September. After that, it would be completely unpredictable as to the rate at which hearing would return. I was told to anticipate first hearing nothing but a jumble of electronic bleeps. These would gradually resolve themselves into sound, and particularly, speech, but it was impossible to say how long this might take. For some people, it is instant but in other cases, it can take over a year. Nevertheless, not knowing what level of hearing I would have achieved with the new system, two months later I was scheduled to fly to Bangkok, where I would meet Rj. We were to visit one of world's greatest sources of inspiration: Nepal and the Himalayas.

October –November 2016

Days 1–3:   Car-cough-any

To a country dweller like me, London is quite enough of a culture shock, without travelling twenty-four hours for more.

An atmospheric departure

I had caught the 5:27 am from mist-shrouded New Milton station on the edge of the New Forest, in order to connect with the Heathrow shuttle at Woking. Now, I stand at the bus stop for the thirty-minute wait, where a suited gentleman tries to engage me in conversation. Hearing has proceeded to return steadily since my implant was fitted two months ago. But though I really work on engaging now, the challenges remain significant when people do not face me, when the wind blows, when I feel embarrassed at not hearing. So many challenges from this silent barrier; so much that other people simply do not see and therefore presume is not there. I glean enough to understand that he is flying to Oslo on business, but never discover why, for the effort to communicate becomes more than either of us want at this early hour. He turns to easier conversation partners while I look around as the light rises. Perhaps it is the effort of verbal communication that drives me both inward and outward for the inspiration to write, for writing is surely a solitary process.

The bus journey reminds me why it is that I go to London as infrequently as possible. The traffic is endless and semi-stationary all the way; thirteen miles, one hour.

To be more specific, it is Heathrow that is the first culture shock. As I exit the lift on the departure floor of Terminal 2, I am overwhelmed by the scale of the building. The roof of the five-storey concourse towers cathedral-like above the floors, all of which are simultaneously visible through enormous plate glass windows. The spacious and near-deserted lift plaza gives way to an even more spacious departure hall, swarming with ants, scurrying purposefully about. They cluster round the bright lights of what used to be known as check-in desks. But at Heathrow, we no longer check in at desks. Instead, all we ants must select the machine relevant to our journey, which scans our ant-passports and prints baggage labels for our ant-suitcases. Anthill police stand around, giving the appearance of being helpful. We know their true function is to keep the lines of ants moving, trudging ever forward in service of the ant queen most of us will never glimpse. Our bags are weighed and loaded onto the conveyor belt. The anthill opens its mechanised jaws and swallows them, leaving me wondering if we shall ever see them again. I disclose my cochlear implant to the young ant behind the counter, for I am concerned it may set off the scanners in security. She morphs instantly into human mode, talks unintelligibly into a phone and smiles. There are words, but the smile is enough to say the aberration which is my hearing, has been noted in the anthill mainframe, its implications absorbed and neutralised. I am reassured that I will not disrupt the smooth proceedings of the anthill.

I continue into the departure lounge through a security channel that I do not trigger and proceed to squander two precious hours of my life on a healthy breakfast and *The Telegraph* newspaper. Their supply shortens by the day, these precious hours, yet, still, I make choices based on rituals developed over a lifetime. Newspapers tell me almost nothing I want to know any more. They are filled with wars and rumours of wars that unsettle me to the point where frequently, I must stop reading to dry my eyes; this, and the errings of the grace-fallen, who stumble through the furnace of public disapprobation into the chill of tomorrow's anonymity. Yet, still, I buy them, these newspapers, expending resource imprudently with inadequate evaluation, for they are as much a ritual to me as a first-degree initiation in the United Grand Lodge, or a liturgy to an Anglo-Catholic.

The flight is called. A short walk to the Thai Airways gate brings me into contact with smiles hovering over prayerful hands. It is my intention to sleep the flight away, but I cannot. I share my insomnia with Captain America, who has evidently fallen out with Ironman. Much alpha male dominance ritual is enacted in a carefully choreographed super-pugilism that leaves both protagonists astonishingly unharmed – unlike the wars in the newspapers. I find myself wondering if Captain America reads *The Telegraph*. Ironman has not said.

Eleven hours' sleeplessness deposits me in Bangkok airport, where I experience no culture shock whatsoever. This might be Thailand, but the differences from Heathrow are insignificant. I am relieved to discover that I can still buy as many Cartier watches, Hermes handbags and Agent Provocateur perfumes as I might wish. Here, I meet my dear friend Rj, a healer of profound spiritual connection, and soon we are once more lost in a conversation that has little to do with handbags or American alpha male virility metaphors. Food for the soul; I am making this pilgrimage for edification and learning and I am delighted to find it has started already over a Starbucks coffee in Bangkok airport. Surely, this bodes well for the next two weeks.

I snooze my way through a shorter flight, to be woken by the lowering of the aircraft undercarriage as we descend into Kathmandu airport. A single glance from the window brings me white mountains and a green valley, peppered with well-spaced buildings. Is this Kathmandu or Shangri-la, I wonder? I am as seduced as I am disarmed, despite the fact that we have not yet even landed.

Kathmandu airport is another culture shock. Even the officials' smiles as they point us to lines for visas and immigration. All is small scale, reminding me of how my UK regional airport, Bournemouth used to look fifteen years ago. I could almost expect Biggles to emerge from a side door, complete in a goggled leather flyer's cap and aviator's jacket. But this is the twenty-first century, and we have flown fifty years from James Bigglesworth's racism – at least I hope we have.

As we pass the barrier into Nepal, we are offered prepaid taxis to the city centre – a better idea than negotiating with independent drivers, it seems. Rj heads off to his four-day training course in singing bowl healing, a technique in which I know him to be already expert. I step into my taxi, having mentioned conversationally that I want to take a mountain flight in the next few days. A young gentleman joins the driver in the front with the intention of taking me somewhere I can book it on the way to the hotel. Hmm, was this a wise move? Already, the wheels of commerce are turning and the smiles may be merely pocket-deep.

Nothing could have prepared me for Kathmandu. I have been to Third World cities before, but none have compared to this. As the streets become narrower, so the traffic gets louder. Drivers make little allowance for motorcyclists and pedestrians as we pass both within inches and at speed. Everywhere is commerce. Street vendors weighing onions on the back of stationary bicycles jostle spice sellers offering rainbow-coloured powders, while broom sellers vend witches' broomsticks from ill-lit underground shops. Meat is sold open-air and unrefrigerated on street corners. Garlands of paper flowers hang in profusion over incense, shoes and books in English. And everywhere, an unorchestrated car-cough-any colludes in a sunset chorus of mechanised motion.

Kathmandu street vending

Later, after I have checked in at Mum's Home Hotel and lain for a couple of sleepless hours on the bed, I will venture out on foot, knowing that as a tourist, I am fair game to rickshaw drivers, self-appointed tour guides, restaurateurs and even the unscrupulous 'student' who wants 'only to practise speaking English' on me as I walk. We have fallen into conversation and are proceeding further than I had planned, as the light starts to fade. I see my mistake and turn to retrace my steps, but not before he has requested a donation for the 'orphanage' he represents. He does not think my proffered 100 rupee note sufficient for his 'services', and demands 2,500 rupees from me. My opinion differs and is immutable. It is going to be that kind of trip. As I retrace my steps to Mum's, I resolve to let myself be taken for more than is strictly necessary. Resources here are scarce and I will take away with me much value in what I see, experience, and I hope, learn. In my first few hours, Kathmandu has already begun my education.

At Mum's, a typical Nepali meal costs less than £8.00 and I retire to an early night. Once more, sleep eludes. Still, there's always writing.

Dinner at Mum's

The next day, I am jet-lagged, but decide to explore anyway. I know I am accommodated in the Thamel quarter, which bulges with traffic and micro retail. I want first to visit Durbar Square, which looks to be about twenty minutes' walk away. I study the map carefully but I take a wrong turn and walk in the opposite direction for over a mile. At least I get to see the perimeter of the royal palace. I wonder briefly if I might be invited in for momo (Nepalese steamed buns) and coffee. But the monarch, it seems, is unavailable. He expresses his regrets by way of high walls, topped with razor wire and military personnel who stand by the gates expressionlessly. King Gyanendra Bir Bikram Shah Dev evidently values his privacy as much as I do mine.

I attempt to reach to Durbar Square by way of the busiest of roads, where I notice Nepal, like the UK, drives on the left. But it is the only transport similarity I note, for there are few other discernable rules of the road. There might well be *9 million bicycles in Beijing*, as Katie Melua once sang. But as far as I can see, there is not a single traffic light in Kathmandu. Peaked-capped policemen direct the traffic from raised podiums that declare 'The police, my friend'. I am glad to have such friends, for here, pedestrian crossings are an endangered species. And if you try to cross a road without following the lead of a local, you are likely to become an extinct species yourself. I follow the lead of locals and venture out into the traffic, almost in pigeon steps. Amazingly, as we persist, the motorbikes flow around us, as a stream would pass pebbles protruding from its surface. Being a little less resilient than the average pebble, I am relieved finally to reach the other sidewalk.

Burdened

Eventually, I make it back into the main street-trading area, where the sea of humanity is positively tidal, sweeping in waves from one end of each narrow lane to the other. How anyone sells anything is beyond me. If I stop to look at the fascinating array of bolts of coloured cloth, or brassware, or incense, or tourist trinkets, I am poked from behind. I recommence motion rapidly. Yet, I am alone, distanced by language, skin colour and hearing ability from the broad brushstrokes of humanity that paint the canvas of this culture – family generations walking together; lovers arm in arm; beggars squatting, head down over begging bowls; small children clutching even smaller babies with, I presume, enough bottles of milk to sustain an infant until the planned return of the absent mother. There is an inner urge in me to pour money like confetti in an attempt to help. But I have learned from previous travels that the only difference this makes is a short-lived assuaging of my conscience. The benefit to the recipient is momentary. The little ones will be back in the same spot tomorrow, squatting over the same begging bowls, holding the same babies, who will howl with the same pathos. I want to make a difference but I cannot make a difference. I am a privileged westerner who has grown to adulthood never knowing hunger or significant want. But in this, I am most wanting. I have no solutions. I hang my head in shame over this computer, bought with my inestimable wealth, and wonder how it is that we choose to run our world in this way. Namaste – I acknowledge that in you which is eternal – unless you are the expunged flotsam of a society that wants to pass you by without noting the hunger in your belly and the despair in your eyes. Namaste. Namaste. Namaste. My words are as cheap as your poverty.

Kathmandu is an ocean of commerce

Day 4: I Dreamed my Dream for You

The further I venture abroad, the deeper I travel within.

I am standing in the departure hall of Kathmandu airport once again, waiting for a flight to the mountain. I do not have the physical fitness to trek to Everest base camp, but I will not pass through Nepal without seeing the mountain. I joined the long line for security checks a little bleary eyed and not too confident I will know what to do. That's quite a big deal, given my cochlear implant processor, fitted only two months ago, is as yet operating well short of full capability and foreign voices are difficult to understand. I smile at the gentleman next to me who turns out, coincidentally (or perhaps synchronistically),

81

to be taking the same flight as me; though Nepali, he lives in Washington and this is his first trip home in twenty-five years. He feels even more out of place than I do, he tells me, for whereas I, as a white-skinned foreigner, am expected to know nothing, he is expected to know everything, yet is as ignorant of procedures and customs as I am. But his English is excellent and his accent understandable, so I have stuck with him until the flight is called.

In the departure hall, I am observing that it is only when viewed under the microscope of proximity that we are different – different coloured skin, different languages, different clothing, and different food preferences. Yet, as I look up at an electronic advertising hoarding, I see a young Nepali couple beam down indulgently on their two-year-old son in his 'I -♥-Nepal' t-shirt. The same dreams of love and happiness have brought this couple together as are dreamed by young lovers throughout the world, as were dreamed by my generation and throughout all of history. And now, these stereotypical parents dream their dreams for their son, who, when the time comes, will dream of happiness and love, from which will come another generation to be beamed down upon, indulgently.

I acknowledge ownership of the dream as my human inheritance. Yet, observing it drives me ever inward, to explore why we dream as we do, why we are driven by the same motivators, for I will not accept that we are merely machines manipulated by the selfish gene that wishes only to perpetuate. My universe is a friendly place, as Einstein might say. It has purpose. And when our dreaming is done, what remains is the inner journey, for which the outer journey was only ever a metaphor.

The Mountain elicits much clicking of cameras

In the air, we rise rapidly above the snow line, leaving the warmth of the Kathmandu valley dreaming on below, for our dreams today are loftier. We aviators dream of seeing the mountains and the fabled Sagarmatha, which hitherto, I have known only as Everest. There is much clicking of cameras, not least my own, as we are invited, one by one, into the cockpit for the best views of all.

Sagarmatha from the aeroplane: as close as I will get

And finally, there she is, high and lofty, looking down from her ice kingdom onto her acolytes of lesser peaks and all of irrelevant humanity below. We lesser beings can but gaze in awe. For we see our scale, we tiny humans, in a universe of orbiting planets and spinning galaxies. And we see our scale, we enormous humans, in a universe of orbiting atoms and spinning quarks. I can absorb neither my microscopic nor my macroscopic scale. I can barely perceive my own comprehensive insignificance, nor my unending consequence. These are lessons of lifetimes in a universe built for learning.

Then, all too soon, it is over, and we are touching down on tarmac once more. Lost in thought, I take the departure gate to the car park. On the ride back into the city, my driver asks where I am from in the UK, for he has spent three years in Hastings, learning business studies. I do not ask why, after such training, he is driving a taxi. He and I both know his time is yet to come.

In the afternoon, I stroll to the Garden of Dreams with my new best friend, Philip Roth. Mr Roth has much to teach me about writing, and I devour his novel, *The Plot Against America*, rapidly and with relish. I am pleased to have discovered another Great American Novelist and wonder why we have not been introduced before: so many authors, so much to learn, so little time. After an hour of tuition at Mr Roth's metaphorical knee, I explore this dreaming garden. It had fallen into ruin since its creation in the 1920s and has now been about two thirds restored with the aid of Austrian financial assistance. The guidebook advises me to bring reading material to distract myself from the 'over-amorous' Nepali couples that evidently come here also to dream. I have. They are.

My dreaming done for the day, I return to Mum's Home through the entirely un-dream-like Thamel, musing upon the insights of one of the greatest teachers of all time:

Our revels now are ended. These our actors,
As I foretold you, were all spirits, and
Are melted into air, into thin air:
And like the baseless fabric of this vision,
The cloud-capp'd tow'rs, the gorgeous palaces,
The solemn temples, the great globe itself,
Yea, all which it inherit, shall dissolve,
And, like this insubstantial pageant faded,
Leave not a rack behind. We are such stuff
As dreams are made on; and our little life
Is rounded with a sleep.

The Tempest, Act 4, scene 1

Day 5: Retail Therapy Shamanic Style

Today is Deepawali. It is serendipitous that I find myself in Nepal at this time, for I had not planned it so. But we will think more on the Festival of Lights later when it is dark. In daylight, I plan finally to make it to Durbar Square, having spent the last two days failing to find it, courtesy of ambiguous maps, a near total absence of street signage and my woefully underdeveloped map reading skills. Oh, for a sat nav. But while daylight persists, I am destined to gain feedback (on the basis, you understand, that there is no failure, only feedback). I settle to looking for presents to take home and perhaps, a small memento for myself, should anything suitable catch my eye. Almost instantly, it does, as I settle upon a colourfully painted wooden carving of the word '*Namaste*'. I am five days into this inner and outer journey and already, this is the obviously apt term for it. I am well pleased with my little find when I happen upon suitable gifts for the ladies in my life – t-shirts for the younger ones and an incense burner plus Nepali tea for the older. Retail therapy has lasted all of twenty minutes, combined with photo taking along the way.

But they are persistent, these Kathmandu retail entrepreneurs. I have barely glanced into the window of a shop selling local artefacts when the owner hails me from across the street, weaves an expert path between the lethal streams of motorbikes, and ushers me into his unit. Actually, I'm quite interested to see what is there, so I do not resist. Inside, he insists on showing me virtually every item on virtually every shelf, with the aid of a small torch, as we near the darkened rear of the shop. Much is tourist trivia, but one item alone catches my eye – a string of small bells. I either know or sense (I can't actually remember which) that these have a spiritual use, so I ask to see them. In broken English, which almost everyone here seems to speak, he manages to convey that they are for use in shamanic healing. And now, he has my attention. I begin to settle on an intent to purchase, if they are affordable.

His first mistake is in insisting that he demonstrate their use. He dons three strings of bells and takes out a drum. I request, and am granted, permission to take his picture. Without warning, he begins jumping up and down, banging the drum vigorously while his enthusiastic animation causes much ringing of bells. And then, I see my error. If these are shamanic tools, it is no form of shamanism that I am familiar with – and I have studied shamanism. These are tools for driving away evil spirits that are presumed to be causing ill-health. And now, I am less keen, dramatically less keen, to make this purchase. Instinct tells me this is not good energy – at least, not for me.

He insists on demonstrating his $500 bells

My mistake is in not walking away without speaking further. But I do speak. And fatally, I ask the price. He looks at me, estimating how much I'm good for. "Dollars or Rupees?" he asks, the English having suddenly improved remarkably.

The question itself portends considerable expense. "Rupees," I answer, hoping not to be fleeced quite so much as I might be if I ask for a price in dollars.

"Five hundred," he answers. It sounds awfully low. 500 rupees is about £4.00 sterling. "Dollars," he finishes. I am, to say the least, taken aback. But it gives me my emergency exit, for I would not choose to afford this sum, even if I still wanted the bells.

"No," I respond gently. "That's far too much for me."

I exit the shop to the familiar strain of "How much you give me for it?" It is a line I have heard repeated several times over the last few days. I ignore, and continue to make my exit, setting off back to Mum's Home Hotel.

But it ain't over 'til it's over. I am making my way along the street, away from the shop. I've covered about a hundred metres, when there is a tug on my arm. I turn to confront the owner of the shamanic bells. "One hundred dollars," he says, beaming me a hopeful smile. I hesitate. I really shouldn't have hesitated. I really, really shouldn't have hesitated. Hesitation is a buying signal. I waver. But I do not want these bells at any price. They are not right for me. I visualise them in my home and I'm not happy.

"No thank you," I say and turn and walk away. But the fat lady ain't sung yet. I cover another fifty metres and there's another tug on my arm. "Fifty dollars."

A culturally appropriated symbol of embrace

"No thank you."
Another fifty metres.
Another tug from the tug.
"Thirty dollars."

"Do you really mean that?" I ask, letting an old life pattern get the better of me.

"Yes," he says, taking me by the arm and leading me back towards the shop. But the fat lady is now singing. In fact, her soprano voice is belting out warning arias at full volume. I touch the bell-man on the shoulder.

"Sorry, but I don't want the bells."

Turn.

Fifty metres. A hundred metres. I'm finally half a kilometre away before I hear "Twenty dollars!" But the fat lady has made her priorities very clear and I walk on, ignoring his increasingly desperate pleas. From five hundred dollars to twenty in five minutes and half a kilometre. I know I said I was willing to be taken financially for more than I needed to be in a Third World country, but I didn't mean by that much!

I return to the sanctuary of Mum's for a rest before heading back out to see the lights.

It's 7:00 pm or so and dark outside. The festival is getting going. Everyone wants Lakshmi, goddess of wealth, to enter their homes and shops, so everywhere is brightly lit for her to see her way. On the ground in front of many doorways, brightly coloured powders have been arranged carefully in enticing designs. Some have flames burning in the centre, some have small offerings of fruit. I had seen these powders on sale ever since I arrived and had assumed them to be spices. Now, I see their true purpose. Fascinated, I make my way towards Durbar Square, courtesy of a downloaded Google map and a GPS signal that tries hard to get an incompetent such as me from A to B successfully. But the many squares in this city have multiple routes converging upon them and I am fooled into wrong turns several more times. Finally, finally, finally, I make it. Well, well. Durbar Square has been there all the time, less than twenty minutes from Hotel Mum's Home. Yet, again, I have been walking in circles. But now, I have seen the light. Only, it's dark, and I can't see the light if you get my drift. Tomorrow, I will come back tomorrow when Rj rejoins me. I turn back for the hotel to discover that Mum has also ordained Lakshmi should be made welcome with lights and coloured powder designs on the floor. The gent behind the hotel desk explains that I am Lakshmi. I get the point. I am bringing wealth into his hotel. I feel greatly honoured and say so.

But the elaborate design of coloured powder on the floor troubles me, for in the centre is a large swastika. It has a very negative European connotation to me and I want to understand the coincidence. So, I ask. And I'm told the design is called… 'a swastika'. Its four right-angled arms are meant to represent welcome, drawing in all from north, south, east, and west. And now, it really does have my attention. Though I had not known this, the Internet tells me it has been a worldwide symbol of good luck since the Bronze Age and remains in common use in this part of the world. Feeling the affinity to Nepal that I do, I would very much like to be able to use it. But after its near hundred-year association with genocide, how could I? Slightly saddened, I shall write the matter off to cultural insensibility, a question of form that I seek to dig well beneath in my pursuit of substance. But I find myself wondering if I will have an appointment with this beloved symbol somewhere further down the road. Tomorrow, I am told, is another day.

Namaste.

Day 6:   Sounds of Silence

My old friend Rj has arrived, bouncing with energy from his training course on the deeper applications of singing bowl resonance in sound healing. We discover we have both been thinking independently of doing the same thing with the day – visiting the Swayambhunath stupa that lies on the edge of the city. We accept the taxi driver's appealingly low fare of 300 rupees (about £2.35) and head off, deep in conversation, to be deposited at the foot of the eastern steps to the temple. The 365-step stairway soars heavenward, rising disconcertingly more steeply as it approaches the summit. I had had some concerns before making this trip that Rj would be rather fitter physically than me and had stepped up my New Forest walks in anticipation. As it turns out, it's the other way round. He's in good physical shape generally, but he's seven years older than I am at sixty, and beginning to feel the challenge that age sometimes brings to the hips. We take the stairs at a manageable pace, stopping periodically to drink in the panoramic view over the city. Signs of earthquake abound throughout the city, and not least of all here, with hastily filled gaps in the stairway, cracks in walls, piles of bricks.

As we climb I find myself thinking of the construction of the stupa: the labourers who hauled the construction materials up this steep hill, the craftsmen who fashioned the carvings that line the stairway. My eye lights onto a carved peacock and I imagine the architect who conceived it, the craftsman who spent who knows how long creating it, wondering what my role was in the temple construction, for there is an overwhelming awareness of having been here before. But it comes with no specific past life memory, so I proceed on upwards, knowing for a certainty that consequential learning awaits me at the top.

The dome of the stupa, its all-seeing eyes, the gold foil, the prayer wheels, all impress the pilgrim, as they are intended to, of his small place within the world. We proceed clockwise round the dome in time-honoured fashion, reaching out periodically to spin the prayer wheels and touch the unseen of heaven. Rj seeks for a particular bowl shop, owned by the relative of a good friend. He has already bought many bowls on this trip but without anything being said, we both know he is going to buy another in this shop. The shop is located, but the friend's relative is absent. We are shown the bowls. As Rj briefly plays several in turn, his mastery becomes as obvious as his reasons for rejecting cheaper bowls. All, though fitting to their use and price, pale into insignificance to the one bowl he settles on. I can feel dramatic vibrations resonating in the air about it, as its pure and exquisite note fills the room, clearly audible, even to me. The transaction is agreed and completed to many smiles, photographs and *Namastes*. As we leave, I express a slight regret that we cannot both buy this bowl, only momentarily though, for it belongs in the hands of a master. Rj will take it home to use in the sound healing he practises and teaches throughout Southeast Asia. For this and his many other bowls vibrate at frequencies that resonate with human chakras, bringing peace, healing and self-awareness when used by an expert such as Rj.

The master sound healer selects a singing bowl

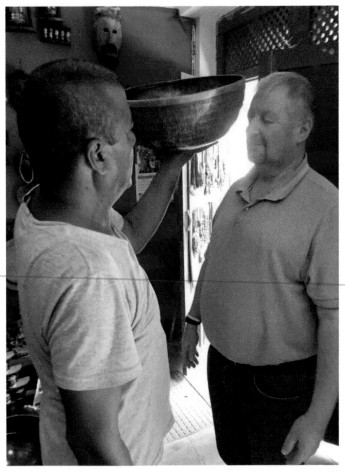

Singing to the solar plexus

But now, Rj wants to find me a bowl. I have one at home, but the idea of buying one feels right. I do not expect ever to teach as he does, but it is time to take the use of sound vibration to the next level in meditation. We step straight into the adjacent store, where bowls literally litter the floor. The proprietor spies the possibility of transaction, and passes me a smaller bowl. But it plays dull and its energy is flat. Rj and I look at each other with negative expressions. A larger, more expensive bowl is handed to me. The same inadequacy demonstrates itself. Nothing is going to match the resonance, the purity of the bowl in Rj's backpack. I have already concluded this transaction is not going to take place and turn to Rj to say as much, when I am stopped mid-sentence with the note coming from behind me. This is utterly and totally different, though I do not yet have the experience to understand why. We look at each other wide eyed. I ask for closer sight of the bowl that has just been struck. The proprietor bids me stand in front of him, gently strikes the bowl once more and I drink down the vibrations from crown chakra to base. The effect is astonishing, as I feel the sensation in each chakra in turn, particularly, in brow and solar plexus. This transaction has already been completed. This bowl is coming home with me, even if I have to carry it on my head through customs.

However, I am careful, for this is when it is easiest to over-pay. Leaving resource in a Third World country is one thing. Being fleeced, as I have already discovered, is something totally different. "How much is the bowl?" I ask, looking the proprietor unswervingly in the eye. I ignore the spiel about how wonderful and expensive it is and how today he is going to give me a special price as I await the figure. $900. The bowl tells me it costs $600. I tell the proprietor. He looks aghast and shakes his head sorrowfully. I need engage no negotiating skills, for I know beyond any uncertainty that this transaction has already been completed at $600. Eye contact does not falter. I repeat slowly, "This bowl costs $600." He responds with less than good grace that he will reduce to $800. "This bowl," I repeat, "costs $600." I am rewarded with a reduction to $700. My words do not change. Rj stands well back, not involving himself in the transaction going on in front of him. Quite suddenly the proprietor agrees $600. Later, Rj tells me his is more than surprised that the seller was prepared to drop so far. He tells me I have achieved outstanding value. I know only what I said, only what the bowl told me. "This bowl costs $600."

Back at the hotel, Rj measures the notes of the bowls electronically and tells me my new purchase vibrates at the note 'G', which resonates with Manipura, the solar plexus chakra. I'm intrigued, but not at all surprised, for I know that much of my outgoing energy flow proceeds from Manipura, which is typically associated with the ability to establish ideas and plans into reality. At higher levels, Manipura's inclination to the intellectual in us yields to the conveyance of wisdom. What a future to aspire to! So, that is why the bowl wanted to come home with me. We have a future together.

We leave our bowls a little reluctantly in our respective hotel rooms and determine to spend the afternoon at Durbar Square. I check Rj is happy to walk, given his hips, but I had not reckoned with the auditory sensitivity of this sound healer. It is day two of Deepawali and at the end of the lane where our hotel is situated, booms one of the loudest discos I have ever heard (but there again, I've never attended a rave, I suppose!). Rj covers his ears in considerable discomfort as we pass. It's not a lot better all the way down to the square. Unbelievably, the crowds are even denser than I have hitherto experienced and Rj struggles to adjust, as I did three days back. We arrive in some relief at the square and take in the sights against the background of the ever deeper intimacies of our spiritually focussed conversation – his life experiences, mine, past lives, learning gained, learning needing to be repeated. It is pure joy to engage at this level with a fellow traveller, once more. We proceed back to the hotel by a longer and somewhat less densely populated route, to dine satisfyingly on steamed rice, vegetable curry and papad, infused with the same profound, edifying and challenging conversation. We feed each other, this old friend and I. After a period alone, the company of a spiritually aware friend feels like an oasis in the desert.

Early retirement follows. As I remove my hearing processor, the sounds of silence open up a welcome space. I fall asleep wondering if Rj is still having to cover his ears to the sounds of the celebrants outside.

Day 7: It is Better to Give...

Is it really a week since I left home? I have to check the calendar to be sure, and yes, this is indeed my seventh day. I wake late, having been writing, reading and meditating during the night. Sometimes, it is incongruent for me to follow traditional sleep patterns. Consequently, we go to breakfast late and there are few people.

As Rj and I sit down, a western lady at the next table smiles and says something to Rj that I don't quite catch. Such encounters happen a lot to Rj, I observe. A conversation ensues about our respective reasons for being in Nepal, and by consequence, our respective occupations. Monica (the name the lady discloses) tells me she visits every year. Together with two friends, she raises funds for an orphanage. And now, she has my attention, as undivided as did the vendor of shamanic bells, but to better outcomes.

It was necessary to move the orphanage into a new building following the earthquake, says Monica, requiring that they raise £35,000. But they have raised over £180,000, opening the way for the children to move into a new 'dream building', as the website puts it. Having elevated the standards of the one orphanage to an acceptable level (decent sanitation, no overcrowding, no mould on the walls, no blocked drains), she continues, they have now identified another orphanage in much worse condition than the first. I am as certain I must make a donation to this activity as I was yesterday that the singing bowl was coming home with me. You can find out more about ADM Nepal Charitable Trust at www.admnepal.org.uk. Please donate. Please donate a lot.

We have determined that today, we will visit Boudhanath Stupa – or revisit it in Rj's case, for this is where he has spent his first four days taking further training in singing bowl healing. Today, it is difficult to book a taxi, for it is a day of increased celebrations for Deepawali. As we eventually locate transport and make our way out to the stupa, the taxi driver tells us the crowds will grow even greater for the next few days, for the President of India is due to visit. Rj is dismayed. Crowds do not work for him. We determine to escape the city to the nearest national park first thing tomorrow morning. Details are arranged with the taxi driver who drops us at Boudhanath. As we enter the monument, the roaring city is instantly becalmed into an oasis of peace as hundreds of tourists and pilgrims quietly circle the stupa clockwise, spinning prayer wheels.

We enter a shop selling crystal prayer beads. Rj chooses a string of black agate. I am not so minded, for I have worn no jewellery since my twenties, disliking the sense of hard objects against my skin. But as he chooses, my attention shifts to a lapis lazuli pendant. I consider carefully, for I seek to avoid impulse purchases now, even in the case of small items. The questions I habitually ask myself are 'Why do I want this? Will it enhance or retard my journey?' The inner answer is surprising. I want it because the energy around me is changing, and yes, this stone is indeed on my route map. I buy. I have long been aware that my journey is taking me in directions I could never imagined. But change brings the opportunity for newness and growth. I am open to change. I am open to growth. I am open to the journey's moving into new territory.

As we circumnavigate the stupa, a monk stands in the broad pathway with a silver bowl from which he is throwing food for the pigeons. Their flocking about him draws attention. I, among many, want to photograph him. There is no restriction, but Rj tells me that it is appropriate to donate if I photograph and I am pleased to do so. I drop a note into the bowl and the monk speaks to me. Not hearing, in my habitual fashion, I lean forward, and touch his aura at his upper left arm (but not his body) with my right hand. He is unperturbed. He repeats his question, which relates to my country of origin. I tell him and he raises his hand, murmuring a blessing. I lower my head to receive it. As I return, Rj tells me one must never touch a monk, for it is a gross insult. No, not even his aura. Chastened, I continue my circumnavigation. There is so much I do not know. So much learning I have yet to derive. Lifetimes of learning lie ahead, even if this is merely a cultural issue, for we are all touched by deeper cultural root than we realise, for reasons we have yet to fathom.

My teacher for this day

We proceed into a bowl shop. It is owned by the person from whom Rj has bought his bowls several days previously. I spy a small book in English that will explain singing bowls to me better than my present elementary understanding. I take it down but am dismayed that the cost is R2,000 – about £18.00. This is more than I want to pay. But as I turn to leave, the proprietor tells me he wants to give me the book. I am astonished. Never in circumstances such as these, a Third World country, a religious monument, has such a gift been offered to me. I accept the return of energy, marvelling once more at how the cycle works. In perpetuation of that cycle, I leave a further sum, asking him to donate it to the cause of his choice. He writes upon the note and sets it clearly aside from his takings from sales.

Today, I have been reminded it is better to give than receive. Today, I have learned that I can give nothing, for the energy is not mine. And the energy of the gift always finds its way back to reenergise me, even if I do not always recognise it when it arrives. Bread cast upon the waters always returns.

Namaste.

Days 8–11:   You Give Me Fever

For two days, the words have not flowed smoothly. As we left Kathmandu, I could feel an infection building and have needed to devote much energy to supporting my body in addressing it. We have left the city for Nagarkot and the mountains, wanting to avoid the crowds for the rest of Deepawali and the visit of the President of India. By night time, the fever has taken hold.

I wake in the darkness, outside my body but still inside my aura. I thank the infection for the Learning it has come to bring. I thank my wonderful body, which is all but on fire as it contains the infection, and drives it out, once the Learning has been delivered. I see much in this heightened awareness than hitherto, I have not seen. Yes, the journey incorporates the words I channel and sculpt. But it is far deeper. This journey is towards the throne room and I am challenged as to how far I am willing to go. The ultimate question is, will I, or perhaps more correctly, when will I abandon my fear? I am in awe. It is my ego that fears to venture forth into rising levels of awareness. Yet, this is a place where no angel fears to tread. There is no compulsion. Only a realisation that there must be a relinquishing of the old security blankets of identity, a willingness to let go of the self, to place the self at risk if I am to step forward to embrace that which is offered.

There can be as many trips around the old mulberry bush as I want to make – "If you want to," as my Guides repeatedly put it, "if you really need to." But the question remains the same as posed when I was at home in the New Forest. Do I want to? Do I really need to? Or am I ready to lay down the rags I previously considered regal garments, in order to inherit the robes of sanctified awareness that I am being offered? 'Love, thou knowest,' I answer as my body burns. To burst forth into the Light requires that I am ready to give up everything I ever held dear, ever knew, or thought I knew, everything I ever valued, in order to be clothed in the awareness that infuses, energises, conjoins, rejoins love to Love.

The next morning, the fever has gone and I thank my body once more, noting now that the time approaches when I must honour it more than I have done hitherto in this lifetime.

At Bagmati: no angels fear to tread

The mountains are close, soaring above the foothills where our hotel is situated. These alone rival most of the mountain ranges I have seen before – the Alps, the Andes, Snowdonia; but oh, the Himalayas. Neither words nor photographs come near to doing them justice. The only way to know them is to be here. I am privileged beyond measure to feel the steady pulse of their energy. For these mountains lend new meaning to the cliché, 'as old as the hills'. Their old, old vibration, their permanence juxtaposed with my transience, rekindles my awareness of my youth and smallness in the eternal context. For this moment, they are gentle, these ancient ones, feeling no need to flex their muscles but when they do, beware. In 2015, they shrugged their shoulders. Fissures opened. Towns and villages were flattened. Thousands died. Yet, for now, these august and revered elders feel less the need to assert themselves, drawing the energy seekers of the world to their foothills, their icy paths, and for the few, their peaks. You do not conquer Everest or Annapurna. You do not assert yourself at them. You infuse their souls and work congruently with them as you climb. At least, you do if you wish to return alive. My friend Chris, Rector of Totton, is experiencing this right now as he journeys to the half-way point up Everest, raising funds for a major church project. But Rj and I do not travel thus. We have other peaks we must ascend.

So it is, that as master of little and apprentice of much, I approach the Namobuddha monastery in Bagmati.

We have hired a driver/guide, Krishan Gopal, whose driving skills we hugely appreciate, as we cross roads so barely worthy of the name as to lend a whole new meaning to the term 'unpaved'. Potholes, more holes than pot, are avoided as oncoming vehicles are engaged in a slow motion waltz of the planets. There are no accidents. No one tumbles from the unfenced edge, down into the valleys far below. The sacrifice of thousands has been enough. As Bruce Willis is famous for saying, "Nobody dies today."

We arrive at the monastery to encounter a group of monks taking a coffee break in the adjacent café. Why not? No one comments or considers it incongruent when I take a break from writing at Costa Coffee back home. Reminded that spirituality is lifestyle and lifestyle is the Journey, I follow Rj and KrishanGopal into the temple of the monastery. We shed shoes and shells. Forbidden to take photos, we approach the Buddha, passing silently the ornate entrance doors, the drums, the brightly painted prayer stools, to infuse the energy generated by the devotion of countless souls. 'Namaste,' cries the heart, 'Namaste, Namaste, Namaste.' I acknowledge in you that which is eternal. I draw near to the God who is in the soul of each of us. I acknowledge myself a part of the same whole, the living universal, the ever present, the alpha and omega, the all, and only.

Roads more hole than pot

Namobuddha Monastery, Bagmati

As we emerge and re-boot, after this, all will be prosaic. The night is spent at a hotel where dinner is wired in series not in parallel. Each item appears in sequence, all of mine before any of Rj's. The whole process takes two and a half hours. We look at each other and shrug. This is Nepal. I ask for coffee. The instant powder is spooned into my cup without hot water. Water must be requested separately as an item in its own right. The next day, we discover the chef has left in a hurry. I'm tempted to ask if he left before or after our meal last night, but I refrain. This is Nepal. We do things differently in the UK.

We spend the following day at Baktapur, cultural capital of Nepal, whose architectural supremacies are extensively and better iterated elsewhere than I can achieve here. As we travel towards it, we engage in animated, spiritually focussed conversation – Rj's work and mine, our respective Journeys and Learnings, the friends and experiences we hold in common and in contrast. Later, as we travel back to the hotel over roads less teeth-jarring than those we traversed yesterday, we fall silent. My attention switches back to the inner Journey, where Spirit brings me to tears of joy, as the deeper meanings of past metaphors in life and in the writing shine out their hidden messages.

Tomorrow, we shall leave the mountains and return to Kathmandu for packing before flying to Chaing Mai on Sunday. Can Thailand possibly offer as much as this? Can there yet be more to learn, more growth to infuse?

Farewell, my mountains, my lovers, my joy. Farewell, my beloveds. Oh, the Learnings you have granted. Namaste, Namaste, Namaste.

Day 12:   Baggage Free

Last night, we had talked the evening away, the blessed fellowship of shared understanding flowing sweetly between us. Rj had spoken of his appreciation of my writing and his unwavering conviction that the energy is building to a crescendo, a proliferation of spirit outpoured. I hold the intent dear, but remind myself that it happens only when ego stands aside and I make way for the words of Spirit to gush through the conduit. For my part, I tell him of my fascination with the way he connects both to Spirit and to the souls' Journeying around him. Time and time again, I have watched others draw near to him, frequently without conscious awareness of the energy flow that attracts them. Age and sex are immaterial. So many are drawn to the warmth of the burning fire that is Love. I have told Rj, he has Jesus energy, but he does not have the same religious background as I do and it holds no real meaning for him.

As we stand in line for airport security, I watch it happen yet again, as he takes his place in the queue behind a young western woman. She is facing away from him. She turns, unaware of why she is doing so. How often are our actions initiated from the unconscious, attracted to energy without the conscious mind realising? She makes eye contact with him and smiles. I might be tempted to say this is sex appeal. But what is sex appeal other than the magnetism of energy attraction? A conversation ensues; a small interaction that was contracted before either of these souls entered the planet for this lifetime. We lose sight of her as she Journeys forward towards the light, oblivious, I think, to the energy transfer that has just taken place.

And then, it happens. For the first time, it is I who make the connection. We are at the departure gate and this time, it is an Asian man, perhaps twenty years younger than me, who catches my eye. We smile and the conversation starts: the reasons for our respective trips. He is a medical salesperson. I tell him of my books and give him the wherewithal to connect to my website. And before I know it, the conversation has turned to spirit. He tells me he is a Hindu. He tells me of past life beliefs, of his knowledge that we are all the same. "Hindu do not eat cow," he says. And I affirm to him how small and inconsequential are the differences that separate us. We are brethren in Love. Skin colour, culture, religious observances; these are small matters and they do not hold us apart. We know the same God and her name is Agape.

Rj had withdrawn as soon as he saw the exchange begin, for he knew what was happening and wanted to encourage it. The surprise, perhaps, is not that this man talks to me, for Rj has told me it is common amongst the nations of the world to smile and connect. It is only we Brits who hold ourselves aloof by habit of ego, or of fear. The surprise is that I am open to this connection. My British reticence, together with my own hearing limitations (for yes, to understand this unfamiliar speech requires particular effort), has held me apart from connecting to other souls for far too long. But now, it is time to leave this baggage behind as my Journey proceeds. Sooner than I might wish, the Hindu brother and his companion are gone to their flight and we line up for our own departure.

At Bangkok airport, Rj sees me to the transfer desk and leaves, for we are on different flights to Chiang Mai, where he lives. I make my connection with moments to spare, noting and returning smiles all around me. I enjoy the short flight, making notes of my experiences all the while, my spirit soaring into the welcoming arms of the living Agape. Too many words, too much awareness surge through me, of past, of present, and of what is to come, for me to record them here, many not destined for disclosure anyway. Like Mary, mother of Jesus, I keep all these things in my heart against a coming day of outpouring. But this heart of mine is already full; so full to overflowing, am I full.

Tonight I will join Rj at his apartment block's guest

suite, then, from Tuesday, day 14, he will be gone for a few days to connect with the new lady in his life, for his heart too is gushing with possibility. Meanwhile, I shall meet for the first time with the august and hugely accomplished Professor Dr Pascual of the University of Makati, for this lady of immense academic literary learning has determined to support the dissemination of my work in the Philippines. Be still, oh, my ego. Be still. Sit at the feet of an expert and learn.

We land at 9:00 pm. I go to reclaim my bag, only to be told it will not be arriving until tomorrow 9:00 am. This journey has seen me leave my baggage behind in more ways than one.

Days 13–14:   Yin to the Yang

In retrospect, it was predictable. The Yang energy that flowed so freely in Kathmandu was going to be balanced by Yin energy this week in Chiang Mai. But twenty-twenty hindsight, I am told, is the possession of us all. The bag delay was a minimal consideration as it turned out. Thai Airlines couriered it to Rj's apartment the following morning. The real challenges were still to come.

I had met Prof. Pascual, a Filipino academic, online over the summer this year, when I was convalescing from my hearing implant operation. Some writing I had posted had caught her eye, probably the poem, 'Taking Refuge', for this work, addressing the plight of Syrian refugees, had caught the attention of many, internationally. She had asked to see more of my work and much had flowed between us – writing from me, academic feedback from her. She is one of the few who actually understand the literary context of what I write and had said of *Dragonsong*, that nothing like it had been published since Spenser's 'The Faerie Queene' in 1590. I had known that. But I had come across only one other person that knew before this. Prof. Pascual had caused some of my books to be published in the Philippines and my poetry to be converted into an Asian form of drama known as 'Dramatic Speech Choir', of which we have no equivalent in the West. She has gone on record as affording me the astonishing title 'the Contemporary Shakespeare'. You will understand that I go to meet this person, who thinks so highly of the words I am sent, with some trepidation. A tour of Philippines' universities is to be arranged for Spring, 2017.

Rj offers to drive me into town and I accept gratefully. He has mentioned that he rarely goes into the city, for its energy does not sit well with him. As we approach the ring road he becomes uneasy, insofar as he does not know precisely where we are going. We work together on Google Maps, neither of us competent with it (we're the older generation remember), and I watch helplessly as he grows more uncomfortable. Finally, we arrive at the hotel, Rj much affected by the discomfort of the environment, me, unable to help. I have learned how carefully this healer guards his centred state from which the healing resonance flows and how easily it can become unbalanced if he does not. A brief introduction follows and Rj withdraws to the greater comfort of the countryside, leaving Prof. Pascual and me to get to know each other.

It quickly comes to feel that we are old friends, for the admiration is clearly mutual. And I discover that my spring tour has now expanded from four universities to seven (it will rise still further before I leave Chiang Mai), incorporating at least two significant conference speeches. Can I really be the person Prof. Pascual believes me to be? We spend an enjoyable day exploring our common ground and the city. Around 5:00 pm I decide it is time for me to return to Rj's. It is then that the real challenges begin.

I have a card with the destination address and a cab is called from the reception of Prof. Pascual's hotel. There is discussion I do not hear between the cab driver and the receptionist as to the destination. It transpires that the telephone number on the card is unobtainable. I press the driver on the matter but he claims to be certain of the location. Later, I am to learn that cab drivers will not admit to not knowing an address, for it constitutes a loss of face. I eye the card carefully. It is beginning to look like my only lifeline in a sea of uncertainty that is growing worryingly rough. We drive for forty minutes before the driver finally admits he has not a clue where he is going (and this after several stops and phone calls to try to get directions). We return to Prof. Pascual's hotel. I am now feeling severely disturbed. If it's hard enough to be lost in a foreign city when you can hear, think for a moment how it's going to be if you can't. And guess what? The low power light on my cochlear processor's battery is now flashing. I'm not sufficiently organised with this device yet to have thought properly through its limitations. I have not brought a spare battery today.

By Messenger, Rj advises that I should get to the Maya shopping centre which "everybody knows", and which is part way to his home. "Someone there will know the location," he says. I am dubious. It sounds tenuous to me, but I have no other option. Prof. Pascual offers to accompany me, but though I'm grateful, it's not going to help. I take the only option and another cab is hailed, whose driver does indeed know the Maya centre.

Soul food and body food in Chaing Mai

Darkness has fallen outside, and now it falls inside too, as negativity descends upon me. I'm stupid. I'm an idiot. I'm incompetent. I should have left earlier. I should have brought a spare battery. I should never have taken this trip. I'm disabled. Disabled people shouldn't take risks. I should. I shouldn't. I should. I shouldn't. My old friend Mr Negativity is very good at 'should' and 'shouldn't'. Mr

Negativity is a past master at twenty-twenty hindsight. Negativity is a prescriptive, soul-crushing emotion. The only person disabling me is me.

As the cab drops me at the Maya centre, my old mates, Mr Fear and Mr Anger, sidle up alongside Mr Negativity. I'm afraid of ending up alone in a foreign city with no ability to hear. I'm angry at myself; at Rj; at every archetypal cab driver the world over, who is undoubtedly going to try to fleece me of every penny, rupee, baht and cent I own, take the shirt off my back and leave me bleeding at the side of the road in true Good Samaritan fashion. Externally, I remain composed enough to ask at the line of cabs if anyone knows the address on the card I am still clutching. Many pairs of shoulders make many shrugs. In a more centred state, I might wonder if this is the mostly widely understood expression of ignorance in the world. But centred is not the state I am in. At this moment, I am the last word in spiritual disconnectedness.

Finally, someone looks up the address on Google and scales fall from several eyes. "Oh, there!" I guess they're saying.

"Yes, there!" I might well have replied. Instead, I accept the exorbitant charge I am quoted for the trip with a minimum of negotiation. I shriek silently inside, mocking my own stupidity as we drive to the block where I am deposited with a minimum of fuss. I reach the room just before my processor battery fails. I have not stopped to buy supper – I wouldn't dare. It's not going to hurt me to miss a meal. Come to that, it wouldn't hurt me to miss several meals. I try to read but am too disturbed. The light goes out at 9:00 pm and mercifully, I sleep. It will be some days before I can stand far enough away from these deep-rooted emotions to evaluate their meaning.

Wat Prathat Doi Suthep, Chiang Mai

The next day is as full of temple visits as Chiang Mai is full of temples. It's good to draw energy and re-centre. But the city; this city is very, very different from Kathmandu where, despite the press of poverty and people, the learning flowed freely and generously. Chiang Mai is Yin to Kathmandu's Yang, at least for me. It is brash and self-confident, exuding its self-sufficiency on every street corner. I will enjoy the enclaves of energy that are the temples and I will gladly drink down what Spirit sends, but I cannot engage with Chiang Mai in the way I have with Kathmandu. Kathmandu wraps in heartfelt embraces; Chiang Mai nods its acknowledgement inscrutably. I miss the warmth of a poverty-laden people, who share freely all they have and welcome travellers into their hearts and homes. A visit to Chiang Mai will be courteously pleasant and I am glad I have come. But I know I will not return – or if I do, the city will be avoided, for I will be coming only to embrace old friends who possess Yang energy that balances the city's Yin.

And thus it is, that into my incongruence, dawns election day. The world as I know it, as we all know it, is about to change forever.

Day 15:   Dow Kowtows to Tao

It is the day of the 2016 presidential election in the USA. Worldwide, Lightworkers have eyed the campaign and the horrendously difficult choice our American friends have to make with growing unease. Results are due around midnight GMT. In Thailand, I am seven hours ahead. As dusk falls, I check my iPhone repeatedly for the BBC news. If there's one source of journalism I can rely on in this world, it's the BBC. Long may it be so. The results duly filter in as the witching hour approaches. Clinton leads. Trump leads. Clinton needs 170 electoral college votes to win. Trump needs 47 votes to win. The results play a macabre game of leapfrog as the candidates wrench the lead from each other, drawing ever nearer to the winning post. (First time round I mistyped that as 'sinning post'. Perhaps it wasn't a mistype.)

I am no particular friend of Hillary Clinton and the Democrats. As a former entrepreneur, I have a particular loathing of the regulatory environment which Donald Trump is committed to sweeping away, for in my opinion, it emasculates wealth creation. It was this destructive force that finally garrotted my own business so ignominiously two years ago. It is not the prospect of Donald Trump personally as president that concerns me, however obnoxious I find the man and his prescriptions for the supposed ill-health of America and its economy. What disturb me profoundly are the hitherto latent forces that such a presidency will unleash. Once in post, the man will surely be reined back by practicalities, the common sense of the team around him and the daily cares of office. Nevertheless, there is a perniciousness hovering. It has hung silently in the darkness for seventy years, rarely permitted to raise its head into public view. But now, we have forgotten the learning of my parents' generation. We have forgotten what the EU was set up for and we have forgotten why the United Nations was established. We have forgotten why a world war was fought. Worldwide, those reasons have disappeared into a bureaucratically inspired barbed wire tangle of mindless controls that benefit few outside the regulatory 'Establishment', who thought it their destiny to rule the world in perpetuity. Our ignorance of lessons learned by former generations and our exhaustion at the demands of the tentacles of politically inspired control have caused a seismic shift. New paradigms are in the making before our eyes. Middle America has spoken and it knows not what it says, nor where those pronouncements will lead.

As the final result becomes obvious, I weep. I weep for my friends in ethnic minority communities in the USA. I weep for America. I weep for all of us. Yin energy is on the rise, and that rise will be astonishingly rapid. World events unfold that need no further telling here, for they will be remembered and recorded for the generations. I watch the stunned Facebook posts. I watch the news as it is reported. The world has become instant in our generation. There is nothing we do not know in the moment, should we wish to know it. And the atmosphere is all but post-thermonuclear. In cyberspace, people are, as it were, wandering round in a daze, wringing their hands and wailing, and me? As yet, I do not know what to do either. I turn out the light, for the light has gone out.

Days 16–17: Elephants on My Bed and Hornets on My Path

I have left the city centre to spend my last two days in an oasis of peace called Kireethara Boutique Resort. It is by far the best of the five hotels I have stayed in on this journey and it is a relief to have a little comfort as the trip winds down. Here, there are elephants on my bed (fashioned from the towels, you understand), a bathroom with a walk-in shower and a small patio, should I choose to use it. I prefer the air conditioning, the temperature being a 'mild' (for Thailand) thirty-two degrees.

Elephants on my bed…

In reception is a sign offering Thai massage. I have seen many massage boutiques in the city but have not been drawn. Other Learning has taken precedence. Here, it feels different. Over lunch, I check the moral suitability of the offering with Rj, who assures me that there will be no compromise. I book. The masseur, an attractive young Thai woman who speaks English, follows me to my room, where I explain my hearing limitations once I remove my processor. She arranges me supine (and clothed!) to her professional satisfaction on the super king bed and gets to work on my left leg. I had heard the technique would be intense and I am not disappointed. By judicious use of angles and counterbalance, more pressure is applied to my tired limbs than seems possible for one small young woman to achieve. As she progresses round my legs and arms clockwise, the process is not without pain, but oh, so enjoyable as muscle tension is released and the muscles themselves re-oxygenate. With the deep, steady pressure, I close my eyes and slip into trance. Images slide before me, coalesce, then fade. I think about the memories we store in the neurology of the body, the black bags of Ho'oponopono. I watch as the old slides away.

Rj joins me for the most Thai of Thai meals – hot soup (and there really needs to be a more extreme word for it than hot) and old eggs, preserved I don't know how (for my ignorance, if they used the term, they would call me a Philistine). But it all tastes remarkable and the evening slips into the easy fellowship we have come to enjoy. We both recognise clearly the quality of connection we have established, and how our respective missions will help each other. We are full of wonderful anticipation for the future. But I remain troubled, for outside our oasis of calm, the energetic balance of the world is changing more rapidly than most of us could ever have expected.

I sleep a few hours and am woken by a consequential dream. These dreams have been few in number over this lifetime, less than ten in total, but always heralding significant change. And in this one, Rj and I are ascending the gentle slopes of a mountain, accompanied by many other Lightworkers in buoyant mood. Ahead, I can hear the sound of someone keyboarding and I know he does not have long left before passing over. I must reach him before he does. Rj and I leave the gaiety behind and proceed on. He takes a moving stairway upwards. I walk parallel to the stairway, struggling my way over ground covered with white quilting. As I approach the summit, I am distracted by the appearance of a large black and yellow hornet. I'm disturbed by childhood fears and recollections of stinging insects. I see more hornets and though they are ignoring me, they distract me from the task in hand. I finally realise that the insects are emerging from the same place as the keyboarding. If I want to reach the typist, I'm going to have to ascend above my fear and pass through the hornets. In the dream, I turn back and say to Rj, "There's a bit of a problem." But now, I am awake and pondering the meaning of the dream. I write up this travel log at 3:00 am and check the detail of Ho'oponopono on the Internet. If you are not familiar with this Hawaiian healing and balance restoration methodology, check it out. I am reminded of the four steps: repentance for causing whatever ails; a heartfelt request for forgiveness; the expression of gratitude; the expression of love. I run through the practice in connection with a personal presenting issue, knowing that this process will move to centre stage in my experience and practice now. For if I perceive ill in the world, I am responsible and have the power to heal – we all do. I will channel the healing with words – words are my calling. In so doing, I will heal and be healed simultaneously. The hornets of my own fears and limitations will not stop this now. I will ascend through them to the summit, to the typist whose keyboarding is summoning me. I will reach him before he passes over.

We are due today to visit the hot spa at San Kamphaeng where the water gushes from the earth at a little over boiling point; hot enough that people buy baskets of eggs from the many stalls to boil in it. Here, as everywhere, the mourning for the lately deceased Thai King is in clear evidence. Rosettes at the entrance are black. People dress in sombre clothing. Behaviour is less than exuberant. This nation revered and loved its King deeply: an admirable sentiment that all too often cannot be echoed in our western world, which commonly exhibits excessive behaviour amongst the privileged.

We each take a private hot bath in the mineral waters (said to be good for the joints and the skin, even if it does leave you smelling of eggs!) and later wander over to the spring itself. I note that there are no barriers to prevent people approaching the scalding water. My mind is attuned to western notions of health and safety. Here, individuals take responsibility for their own welfare. It resonates back to the election result.

As Rj takes my photo in front of the geyser, others are doing the same. Quite suddenly, a young woman takes my arm and motions her boyfriend to take her photo with me – a gesture that simply would not take place in the West. It has no sexual connotation. It is simply friendly. I return the compliment and take a picture for her and her boyfriend on their camera.

On the return journey, I grow quiet, knowing these are my last few hours in Thailand. This journey, these Learnings are nearly at an end. Yet, it troubles me that I have not yet discerned the meaning of the dream –- until in a moment, all becomes clear. The hornets and the typing emanate from the same source. They are Yin and Yang, two aspects of the same reality. One is not to be feared and the other pursued, for both are my inheritance and one cannot be had without the other. It is fear that needs to be relinquished, childhood fear and perceptions learned from others.

I can pass through the hornets now. Whether they sting or not is immaterial. It is my Journey and it is exactly how it is meant to be. I can press on and reach the summit. I can, and will, meet the typist before he passes from this life, for I am him, and he is me.

Kathmandu, Nepal and
Chiang Mai, Thailand
November 2016

To Learn, to Love and to Grow

At that initial meeting with Professor Pascual of the University of Makati (UMAK), Manila, I had been invited to visit the Philippines in Spring, 2017, to address a conference organised by the University Circle of Professional Educators (UCPE). The conference was followed by invitations to speak in several universities in Manila where I was repeatedly afforded a welcome fit for royalty, speaking to audiences of hundreds and, in one case, thousands.

Whilst in Metro Manila, it was impossible to ignore the astonishing pace of economic development taking place, evidenced by the rate at which whole districts were being rebuilt with skyscrapers and shopping malls. This had left me questioning who was really benefitting from the economic explosion that is now sweeping this city, as well as wondering the extent to which material benefit was being dissipated into the rest of the Philippines.

When I was invited for 2018, to speak to UCPE conferences in Cambodia and Bangkok, followed by a repeat tour of the Philippines, my acceptance of the invitation was a foregone conclusion. However, whilst I would again pour my soul into the stage speeches and seminars so as to give everything I possibly could to my audiences, this time, I planned to pay rather more attention to observing the transformation taking place in the Philippines. And on this visit, I was told we would be taking road trips into less accessible parts of the country. My heart held huge anticipation as to what I might witness and what it would be possible for me to give.

Day 0:   I'm Leaving on a Jet Plane

He's lying on my bed looking doleful. He's not been willing to let me venture more than three metres away from him for the last two days. Preparations for this trip started six months or more ago, but he is not to know that. He cannot tell what I am doing when I am seated at my desk, e-mailing travel arrangements to the other side of the world and back. When he is ignorant of what is about to happen, he is content just to lie at my feet during the day, mug me for after-dinner carrots and nag me to go to bed at 8:00 pm when, he reckons, all respectable creatures should be sleeping. But two days ago, when the big black suitcase came down from the hall cupboard and I started filling it with shirts and socks and meds and sunglasses, that is when he knew, I was going away. I found myself whistling the old John Denver tune, 'Leaving on a Jet Plane'. How am I supposed to tell my best friend I will be away for four weeks and will be back in time for his fifteenth birthday, when my best friend doesn't speak English? He speaks the language of body movement and eye contact, licks and cuddles, love and sadness. In these tongues, he speaks more eloquently than I could ever write. But understanding the meaning of twenty-eight tomorrows? That is a very different matter.

It was in August 2017 that I had accepted the invitation from the UCPE (www.ucpeone.org) to deliver keynote speeches to their back-to-back conferences in Siem Reap, Cambodia and Bangkok, Thailand and then, to fly on to

Manila to spend three weeks in the Philippines, where I had been given such a rapturous welcome the previous year. I love this wonderful, inspiring work. But each day away brings us closer to my boy's final departure, when he will leave his luggage behind and climb the metaphorical aircraft steps for a flight from which he will not return. But not yet, please, God, not yet, and particularly, please, not while I am away.

So, here I am, all but fully packed and a little ahead of schedule, with a free hour to pen what I anticipate will be the first few lines of another travelogue of another odyssey. But I am no king of Ithaca, and at this stage of the trip, my mind is filled with singularly un-regal uncertainty. I cast back to the invitation – *Two* conferences? *Two* speeches at each? What I find myself wondering, is my relevance to an educators' conference at which every other delegate seems to be a Ph.D. who has already published a dozen respected academic papers? And that to be followed by a dozen or more university and school presentations in the Philippines? Last year, I became adept at walking into a lecture theatre with no idea of what I was going to say, and delivering a two-hour interactive lecture on 'What is creativity?' or 'Beauty in literature'. And always, always, the underlying question, sometimes actually spoken by a member of the audience, sometimes only implied: 'How do we get to do what you do?'

My answer was always much the same. "You must learn to open yourself to the silence. You must develop the discipline to turn off the noise of external communication and learn how to recognise the awareness that is already there inside you; to permit that which is yearning, in deep groans of silence, calling to you, to allow it to come out. Furthermore, you have to trust it enough not to question it." This has taken me a lifetime to learn. This is what, for me, the one Journey has thus far been about. It is a Journey that will be shared, in their turn, by some of these dear ones who want to walk the same path. It is the long road, traversed one purposeful step at a time, in the direction of enlightenment. There will be many miles to travel on this path, with much dust billowing about us as we do. It will take many lifetimes to traverse those miles.

Open yourself to the silence

But for now, my own path leads to Siem Reap and Bangkok, where my talks are entitled *Do Androids Dream?* and *The Machine Stops*. Both will be innovative to the academic ear; both can act as ko-ans to minds honed only for critical evaluation – at least, for those that are ready. And then, the conferences will be over, and in the care of my indefatigable itinerary manager, Prof. Pascual of the

University of Makati, I will move on to the Philippines: Manila, Camarines Sur, Ifugao and other places yet to be specified, where I shall give voice to a new presentation, *The Story that Changes Your Future*, for the first time. As soon as I announced that title, a flurry of excited questions came back immediately, as to what ground it covers. And now, I wait with fascination to watch the changes to futures that might follow its delivery, at least for those who are ready for change. 'He that has ears to hear: let him hear.' For like the master teacher who came before me, whom I seek to emulate, however imperfectly, I speak mostly in metaphor. Not all are yet ready for it. Not all yet, have ears to hear.

But before all that, tomorrow, just before 7:00 am, I shall be listening out, with John Denver on my mind, for 'the taxi, that is waiting and blowing his horn. Already, I'm so lonesome I could cry…'

And Matt? He will look at me dolefully again, asking with only his eyes, how it is I can leave him. Twenty-eight tomorrows are twenty-eight too many, when you're almost fifteen years old and your legs ache from arthritis. But in the care of his mum, who loves him like I do, he will remain safe, and lovingly over-fed on carrots and Bonios. He will think of me seldom. I shall be looking forward to returning to him from the moment I leave.

When all the cases stand ready in the hall, and I am preparing for my last night at home, Prof. Pascual messages. Will I fit in one more talk on arrival – at Sunrise? That is Sunrise the school in Siem Reap, Cambodia (http://newhopecambodia.com), not sunrise the time, you understand. But it might as well be the time, since I shall be whisked from the airport to start speaking an hour and a half after I touch down. This is what I love so much about visiting my friends in South East Asia – the unexpected.

Days 1–2:   People Talking Without Speaking?

I arrive at Siem Reap airport and exit the aircraft to be confronted by the wall of humidity that I am so familiar with, in this part of the world. Passing uneventfully through passport control and collecting my luggage (yes, all of it has arrived, oh ye of little faith!), I exit the terminal into a country I have never visited before. A tuk-tuk is summoned, my first journey in such a vehicle. I request a photo with the driver, after which we proceed, me clicking my camera at the new sights that remind me of my visit to Chiang Mai, Thailand, eighteen months back. The roads are emptier, but the architecture similar. Buddhist temples adorned with gold slide past. Pagodas and spirit houses jostle modern hotels, for Cambodia is investing much in attracting tourism. I hope they are careful to preserve their culture as they throw themselves headlong into enticing tourist-dollars into their land.

My knowledge of this country is outdated. I have paid inadequate attention to it since the 1970s and the vile era of Pol Pot and the Khmer Rouge. I shudder at the memory of the indescribable depths of evil to which the human soul (or at least some human souls) is capable of descending. But recovery and economic growth are all about me, with much modernisation in evidence, in the form of hospitals, hotels and restaurants. We pass a building site in the early stage of constructing a western-style shopping mall. I hope, without expectation, that it does not become filled with western junk food outlets, such as seem to stand for progress in other places I have visited in Southeast Asia.

A brief stop to drop bags at the hotel is followed by an immediate departure for the Sunrise Foundation, an Australian-originated educational charity. In Cambodia, the authorities provide the land for schooling, but the building and running of schools have to be privately financed. Here, too, building is rapidly advancing. Though present capacity is largely limited to tin-roofed, single-storey teaching blocks with open doorways and unglazed windows, it is evident that soon there will be a fine complex of new, multiple-storey buildings on this site, serving the needs of generations of schoolchildren to come.

I am introduced to a classroom of forty or so white-shirted teenagers. I have had no time to prepare new material and am unsure of how good their English actually is. Limited westerner that I am, I speak only English and my verbal communication fails when others cannot address me in my own language. I make the excuse that I cannot hear much in English, even with my new cochlear implant, so other languages would be next to impossible to learn. But I know in my heart that it would be little different if I could hear. Thus, I proceed through an adjusted version of *A Journey to the Land of Risk*, a presentation about connection with one's own inner creativity, that I developed last year for universities and schools in the Philippines. I hope I am making up in movement and body language some of what may be missing in the audience's understanding of the words. I know much of the value of a visit such as this lies in the fact that a westerner has actually taken the trouble to come. I reflect upon the universal reality, that it is primarily by eye contact and body language that we convey to people that we value them. And if there is any conflict between what the body says and what we translate into words, it is the body language that will be believed.

The jet-lagged bedraggled Brit makes a spectacle of himself

Yet, as the words pour forth, I take a little comfort that others gather spontaneously at the doorway to swell the audience. I am hoping that implies I am saying something worth listening to. I could be wrong, though. It might be simply that they want to view the spectacle of a jet-lagged, bedraggled Brit making an idiot of himself. We do well not to think of ourselves too highly. Let others urge us higher up the table, if it is our place so to be lifted. We shall remain at the lowly end, until called upwards by the master of the feast.

Soon, we are done and ready to leave. Later, the photos will tell me just how dishevelled I looked, leaving me wondering exactly when the last time was that I had looked into a mirror. So, maybe, I was right. The attraction was indeed more in watching the unruly-haired Brit perform, than it was in what he had to say.

I remain hopeful that for some, the words of metaphor will sink in. And where the seed falls, later so will rain, and sunshine will follow. Perhaps, there will yet be a wheat field, resplendent with corn.

He that has ears to hear, let him hear.

Days 3–4: People Hearing Without Listening

UCPE is mounting a conference for educators here, as a combined educational and fundraising event. I am to deliver two keynote speeches on consecutive days, before we move on to a larger and more sophisticated version of the same event in Bangkok. But here in Siem Reap, the infrastructure is inevitably more basic, with repeated power breakdowns and more constrained physical resources for conference delivery. It does not matter to me. I will offer the message I have to bring, to anyone who wants to listen, wherever that takes me.

But whilst the physical limitations are no issue, the

English language capability is much harder to deal with. We try working with an interpreter, but give up part way through the presentation. My talk, *Do Androids Dream?*, explores the challenges of skill transfer in a world that makes knowledge redundant almost as fast as it is learned. But this is not an easy concept to convey in translation, and I have pitched the level of the speech based on my experiences in the Philippines last year. This is a mistake. The talk misses the mark. Other speakers, whose deliveries are much more on practical teaching resources and how to access them, have an offering that is much more obviously relevant to teachers in the Siem Reap of 2018.

Come the night, sleep eludes me for reason of jet lag. I manage about two hours, adding to the effect of sleeplessness on the journey from the UK itself. At this stage, all I can do is hope I can sustain, for I seek to make up by energetic delivery what is lacking in comprehension of content.

By day two, I am concerned that the second speech will go the same way. *The Machine Stops* (the title, of course, having been borrowed from E. M. Forster's short story of 1909), is actually a metaphorical exploration of what happens when a society obsesses with technology. The key phrase in the speech, 'To Learn, To Love and To Grow', is immediately latched onto as a focal point for the educational process in which these folk are involved. At coffee break, much appreciation is expressed, many books are bought and signed (intriguingly, mostly my dystopian future-set novella, *A Home For Other Gods*) and many photos taken. I am relieved that this time, I have it right. What accounts for the difference is impossible to say. "We does what we cans," as Roald Dahl's BFG so eloquently put it.

The conference is brought to an early close because we have a flight to catch to Bangkok; but not before a major exercise in certificate presentation is undertaken, accompanied by much applause and more picture-taking. I have learned to hold a smile, unbroken, for a full fifteen minutes now. Is this, I wonder, an authorship skill?

More tuk-tuks are summoned and we depart for the flight. As the wind flows past me, I observe the enormous numbers of hotels that line the main highway out to the airport, completed, under construction, or merely announced on billboards as yet to come. On the road, though cars are well in evidence, the motorbikes and tuk-tuks make up maybe 80% of the traffic. With the immense pace of economic growth in evidence, I am wondering how long it will be before four-wheeled vehicles are in the majority, and before private drivers outnumber tuk-tuks. By that time, these folk will no doubt have increased their income, both nationally and individually. But if care is not taken, Siem Reap will go the traffic-infested, fume-choked way of so many other Asian cities. Nevertheless, I observe that virtually all road users are respectful of the 40kph speed limit. This bodes well for a sensible approach to road use. The future actually looks quite promising for Cambodia. I very much hope that I will be able to return for a longer visit on another occasion. There is something soft, something warm and inviting in the spirit of this people. I would like to know more of them and their national journey.

At check-in, I realise with a jolt that I have left my coat at the hotel. Worse still, the coat contains my spare batteries for my cochlear implant, without which I will be close to profound deafness. I've told myself before, I must never forget I am deaf – the implications, particularly in a foreign country, can be devastating when the technology cuts out for lack of power. I've told myself a dozen times, a hundred times, but I obviously do not listen. I look sheepishly at my companions, Prof. Pascual and Gerry Motsinger, who make phone calls and send Messenger messages. Soon, the problem is resolved. My friends Art, Jen and Jioff return to the hotel, retrieve it from the storage room and bring it to the airport to follow on a later flight. Through in the departure lounge, I find Costa Coffee. In a John Wesley moment, my heart is strangely warmed at this sight from home. Naturally, I avail myself of its offering.

Despite my one-man attempts at self-sabotage, the tour is going well.

Days 5–6:   One Night in Bangkok

Arrival in Bangkok in darkness on this, my first visit to the city, discloses that they drive on the sensible side of the road, that the motorway into the city is as straight as a laser beam and that taxis charge considerably less than they do in London. On the ride into the city, my mind drifts back to the old Tim Rice-Björn Ulvaeus musical, *Chess*:

One night in Bangkok makes a hard man humble,
Not much between despair and ecstasy.
One night in Bangkok and the tough guys tumble,
Can't be too careful with your company.
I can feel an angel sliding up to me.

I've never considered myself a hard man, but humility takes attention to maintain when you are the centre of attention. And as for angels, I feel them with me all the time. Bangkok and I might yet become good friends. I will later discover that only foreigners use the name Bangkok anyway. Thais call it 'Krungthep', meaning City of Angels.

The conference the next day is a more sophisticated event, hosted on the nineteenth floor of the Baiyoke Sky Hotel, the tallest hotel in Southeast Asia. In the manner I am now familiar with, proceedings commence with a doxology and both the Filipino and Thai national anthems. Pride in national identity is something I noticed on my last working visit to Southeast Asia – a trait that is not nearly so well developed amongst my own countrymen and women. We would do well to learn some of the habits of discipline that are commonplace here.

For the second time, I deliver *Do Androids Dream?*, an exploration of how, in a world of unstoppable technological advancement, we fail if we teach only knowledge and skills, for these become redundant rapidly. To preserve our ability to stay ahead of the machines, we must increase focus on teaching at the level of values – curiosity, flexibility, open-mindedness. I wrote the speech in December 2017. At Davos in January 2018, I noticed that Jack Ma, of Alibaba fame, covered similar ground. Who showed him my notes, I wonder? I must ask him next time I see him.

Whilst the conference is well organised and at a sophisticated level technologically, once again my slides do not come up in the right order. Perhaps we have a little more time yet before the machines take over. Lunch is hosted on the seventy-eighth-floor restaurant, which offers breathtaking views of the city. It consists of an international buffet, almost the largest I have ever seen (the Christmas buffet at Raffles hotel in Singapore still pips it to first prize, though). Intriguingly, there is virtually nothing on offer for vegetarians, though. I console myself with the reminder that my body can hardly be said to be in need of food, anyway.

In the evening, I am reunited with my coat (including the vital batteries) by my friend Ony, who has taken it into custody during our enforced separation. It shows no sign of having missed me. Perhaps it has bonded with her now instead. That's ok. It is leather and, having now embraced vegetarianism, I will divorce it soon anyway. A picture from home, which is now shivering at minus 7° C of freak, late season snow, confirms that someone I care about greatly has not forgotten his coat.

The next day, Sunday, is spent at leisure in Bangkok. I decide on a river tour as the best way of taking in the feel of the city. From the river, I catch sight of the Royal Palace. Thais hold their royal family in enormously high esteem – a value I admire, which we have not sustained to quite the same extent in the UK. On the riverbank, modern towers of commerce and domestic living share the space with Buddhist and Chinese temples and mosques. Also in evidence are a surprising number of buildings at the shanty town level. New money is driving out old poverty, but has yet to complete the job comprehensively.

Bangkok from the 78th floor of the Baiyoke Sky Hotel

Chao Phraya River, Bangkok

Shopping in the unending street-markets follows. As evening falls, more street vendors appear. I am offered long skewers of prawns and Thai soup from large metal pots, both of which I decline. It's like an enormous street party. Late in the evening, I am belatedly informed that no accommodation has yet been booked for me in Manila. We are just twenty-four hours away from our scheduled arrival. I raise my eyebrows at the just-in-time approach I see so much of here. It is challenging for me, but clearly works for my hosts. Not to worry. I reach for my iPhone and am grateful I have at least mastered the technology of Airbnb. Sleeping space is secured and I am about to turn in for the evening, when I am informed that a few additional bookings have been made on my Filipino tour. No problem. I was expecting that. "How many events do we have now?"

I ask naively. It's a twenty-one day tour, including travel days and rest days. "Twenty-seven," comes the answer.

Days 7–8:   Come Fly With Me

In the morning, I am up at 4:00 am for departure to Suvarnabhumi airport. The night market is still in full swing, though the street food vendors seem to have packed up and gone home. Eat your heart out, New York. As a city that never sleeps, you ain't got nothing on this.

Arrival in Manila rekindles a bucket load of memories from my last visit to this city of skyscrapers, which is rising so fast. If you're looking for somewhere to invest long term, with a population of almost 100 million, 40% of which is still at school, the Philippines offers potential opportunity. The economy is presently ranked as thirty-fourth in the world, but projected to be the sixteenth by 2050, when it will also be the fifth in Asia. The brand identities we see from the car attest to the foreign money that is pouring in. Whether it is more to the benefit of Filipinos or outside investors remains to be demonstrated. I hope what I am seeing proves to be win-win. I am accommodated on the sixteenth floor of a tower block in Bonifacio. Tomorrow the tour proper starts.

The next day starts at a leisurely pace, due to the fact that the day's presentation begins at 1:00 pm. I am intrigued to discover that I am living on a virtual building site, my tower block being the only one of five on the complex that is actually complete. All around me is raw concrete, glass awaiting installation and dust, so much dust. The few remaining slums I can see from my window are apparently being cleared rapidly to make way for the tower block. My tower has forty floors and I count twenty-four apartments on each floor. "Do the math," as my American friends would say. Slum clearance, in principle, is good. But I can't help wondering who affords the new apartments. By UK standards, they are affordable; by local, hugely expensive, and rising in price every year. I surmise, again, that much investment is likely to be foreign, and wonder once more what the balance of benefit is, between locals and foreigners.

I hit the Starbucks downstairs (true civilisation, of course, existing only where there is Costa Coffee) and note with interest that the cost of a branded coffee is similar to the price in the UK. Given that UK GDP is some thirteen times that of the Philippines, the cost of service coffee is astronomic in local terms. Yes, ok, we must allow for the fact that income is much higher in Manila than rural Philippines. But nevertheless, it remains more than intriguing that pretty much every street corner seems to have a US-branded, or US look-alike, fast food outlet. Western brands are ubiquitous, enticing people to 'live the dream'. On the street, I observe that Filipinos are gaining weight, presumably from the influx of high-processed, high-sugar, high-fat food. Who gains financially though? I'd like to think there is win-win going on here, but I'm uneasy at the possible exploitation of dreams. Modernisation, even when externally financed, brings benefits, for sure. But the benefits comes at a price. Will

Filipinos still feel positive about this journey that they are making in one, or two generations' time? I hope so. I do not anticipate living long enough to find out.

Days 12–13:   People Writing Songs

I'm at the University of Makati (UMAK) again today, for a very special event. The University has sponsored an open competition to write and stage a thirty-minute musical based on my epic fantasy, Dragonsong. There are seven finalists, all of which will be performed today.

For the afternoon's main event, I arrive at 1:00 pm as requested. We are in the 1,000-seater Grand Theatre. But we are on FLT (Filipino Local Time!) and no one is ready to proceed. Everyone but me, of course, knew that would happen. We use the time for photo opportunities and book signings. At 1:30 pm or so, the theatre darkens and the first performance begins. Seven thirty-minute dramatic and musical interpretations of *Dragonsong* follow. I am seated by the judges, all of whom are prominent in their various fields, from academia to popular music. I watch them exchange comments quietly and write furiously. I don't envy them their job: this is not going to be an easy judgement. Finally comes the seventh and last interpretation of Harmony the Dragon. She is dressed in red, with her face hidden behind a mask. This alone would be enough. But when the mask comes off, the audience pulls back in their seats, gasping in astonishment. There is no question. This *is* Harmony. This is how I conceived her.

The actor's behavioural interpretation, supported by stunning make-up, is perfect. Later, the young lady concerned does indeed win the award for best actor. I ask if she is set for a dramatic career. She would surely go far. But no; she is training to be an accountant!

Lea Odchigue as Harmony from Dragonsong:
a musical interpretation at UMAK

The overall winner is announced. I can only agree with the judges, for the performance was superb. The piece went behind the plot of the book and seamlessly entered the realms of author purpose and intent. Bravo, the winning troupe. What a delivery!

Fortunately, the next day is a rest day. Prof. Pascual offers to accompany me out to see the museum of National Artist Carlos Francisco, who died in 1969. Given my encounter with the spirit of Jose Rizal when I was in the Philippines last year, I await most keenly to discover what experience this visit will hold. But before we get there, we visit Angono-Binangonan, a site of Neolithic cave carvings, some 4,000 years old. I learn with interest that it was Francisco himself who drew the site to the attention of the National Museum of the Philippines. Then, it's back into the town of Angono. We are taken to the house of the National Artist by motorbike and sidecar – a first for me. When in Rome… ! At the house, the artwork does indeed strike a chord of artistic excitement but there are no revelations of the scales-falling-from-eyes variety that I experienced with Rizal. Nevertheless, I can understand why Francisco is National Artist. His works document in profound emotion the history of the Filipino people. A young man whom I take to be the curator conducts us round the house. But there's something more about this man; something I can't quite pinpoint. We are on the point of leaving, when I see some large canvasses that are clearly work in progress. A much more modern art than Francisco's but also deep, with an air of significance. I ask who the artist is. The young man acknowledges they are his – he is the grandson of the National Artist, also named Carlos Francisco. I reveal my own identity and a conversation ensues about the common ground between art and poetry. I leave a gift towards the upkeep of the house, a small enough sum for the enjoyment I have been offered today. Carlos is taken aback. In return, he gives me a poetry collection by local artists. It is in Filipino, but Prof. Pascual offers to translate some for me.

We return to the city by minibus for the princely sum of 45 pesos per person (about £0.70). When we are just twenty minutes from the metropolis, we pass some of the most disadvantaged housing areas I have yet seen in this country. Again, I find myself wondering just how far the financial benefits of economic modernisation are reaching. Tomorrow we prepare to leave for the provinces, where I will see this from a different perspective. We are bound for Camarines Sur.

Days 14–17:   Comfort Zones and Risks

So, it's 9:00 pm and we're climbing onto the night bus. Our destination is only a hundred and sixty miles from Manila. It is impractical to fly to this location, as the nearest airport is two hours away, and to catch a return flight, we would have to leave just a couple of hours after arrival. So, I am to experience Asian night buses for the first time. The bus is full of double-deck sleeping compartments. I have never done this before – but new experiences are part of the joy of this trip. I'm able to make Internet connection and respond to messages until the journey begins, but once in motion it's impossible to do anything useful. So, I settle down for however much sleep I will be able to achieve, for I generally do not sleep well whilst in motion. But I'm told we have nine travel hours ahead of us, so I get as comfortable as I can (which is not very, as the berth is not designed with an average-height westerner in mind) and soon, we are moving fast on the freeway heading out of Manila. Twelve million or more people live in the conurbation, which is actually an amalgamation of sixteen original cities that have grown into one another. When the freeway gives over to standard roads, I awake and watch the kilometres slip away into the darkness. Though the road is lit most of the way, it's not possible to see much. Some seven hours after departure, I am told we have arrived – two hours ahead of schedule. We bundle our kit out of the bus and I audit (well, I did start my career as an accountant, you know!) my bags and arms and my legs. All of me is accounted for. A motorbike and sidecar are waiting in the darkness to take us to the motel. That's ok. I did this before. I am an old hand at sidecar riding. I might even progress to the motorbike in due course. Eat your heart out, Barry Sheene.

The room is basic but clean and functional and is equipped with Wi-Fi. Indeed, it even has a shower room. These guys are way ahead of us, you know. They had wet room showers long before we thought of them in the West. Only… how do I flush the WC? Ahh, you have to… but let's not go there! I finally fall into bed at 4:00 am and, mercifully, sleep some more. In the morning, I wake to a cold shower (soft westerner? Moi?) before proceeding to breakfast. Here, I find we have been met by a delegation of eight, courtesy of Marieta Ortile and the Sinuknipan National High School, who are sponsoring this leg of my tour. Many photos are taken to much smiling by this group of star-struck young ladies, who treat me as a celebrity. I'm not sure if the cap fits that well, but here in the Philippines I wear it anyway. Perhaps one day, I shall grow into it.

The morning is recuperation time. The delegation decides I would like to visit the beach, so, we head out to the Putting Buhangin Beach Resort, where the water is transparent, and waves murmur secrets to a lonely beach. Food has accompanied us yet again and at 11:00 am I'm told I want lunch. Actually, these folk ate their own breakfast early, so as to prepare food and get to me by 8:00 am. So, if they are ready for lunch that's fine by me. I'm wholly open to the many new tastes I am experiencing here, but choose to eat only plants, unless avoidance of flesh is impossible. Like the Buddhists, I seek to have compassion on all living creatures, for all living creatures suffer. It is important to me to remain vegetarian, but not important enough to cause offence to hosts who have gone to much trouble to offer me hospitality and value my visit highly. But I am fine. For the little I need to eat at this time, there is plenty available. I have time to return to my room and shower again before proceeding to the first venue, Del Gallego National High School.

Del Gallego is a town of twenty-five thousand, offset from the main road behind a steep bank. It is accessed by a relatively narrow concrete roadway, where much goodwill and advanced roadcraft is required to negotiate passage around oncoming vehicles. Fortunately, most are of the motorbike and sidecar variety and our driver is evidently experienced. We pass through narrow streets of relatively well built houses and small shops that seem an eternity away from the shanty towns and tower blocks of Manila. Alighting from the minibus at the school, even I can hear the sound of the percussion band playing in the schoolyard to welcome us. And what a welcome it is. The audience numbers in excess of four hundred and is seated outside, for the schoolyard doubles as an assembly space. Who wants to be indoors in this climate? But even though a pillar-supported roof shades the stage and audience, it is hot; very hot. I ask if the whole school has turned out, but no, the school roll is a thousand. Nevertheless, this is as big a day for these folk as it is for me. Following the usual doxology and national anthem, the percussion band yields to two troupes of traditional dancers, and a Filipino flute ensemble, much similar to a recorder group in the UK.

I am welcomed and introduced formally and the ever-supportive Prof. Pascual nudges me when it's time for me to speak – I rarely hear enough to understand without this. At the appropriate moment, I step forward on the stage and ease into the now familiar presentation, *A Journey to the Land of Risk*. The talk explores the need to challenge ourselves perpetually in order to stretch beyond the comfort-zones of familiarity if we are to free and give voice to the shackled poet within. Whether the poets express themselves through words, or music, or less obviously artistic activities of parenting, engineering or accounting, they make poetry of our lives only when we connect with them. And for this, we must go beyond the land of Comfort Zone and enter the Land of Risk. My own first entry into the Land of Risk today is presenting in 38° heat. I never did this before. To a westerner from a cool climate, it is, to say the least, challenging.

How do we connect to the poet inside us?

After a few minutes of speaking from the stage, I become aware of the distance between the audience and myself. I am not yet connecting as I wish to. In order to reach these folks' inner poets, to touch their souls, I must step beyond the comfort zone of the stage, and across the invisible barrier it creates. But the only risk here is that the microphone will not work so far from the sound system. I descend the steps and, yes, the amplification holds. As I step into the audience, an audible intake of breath sweeps past me. People don't do this here. And there is applause when with a deafening roar, my own poet leaps forth. Now, I am connecting and the connection is maintained seamlessly for the rest of the afternoon. Eye contact and proximity work wonders in releasing shackled poets.

Forty minutes later, it is time for me to fall silent and make way for audience response in the form of questions and comment. They are almost always slow to begin, for few want to be the first to step into the Land of Risk when it comes to asking questions. But when they do come, they bubble like a brook. Almost all are on theme. "How do we connect with the poet inside us?" "How do we make this music in the spheres?" And more overtly, "How can we be like you?" My task now is to point these folk in the direction of what is already inside them – what has always been inside them. And I tell them, as I tell all audiences, that to find the inner poet, the inner artist, the inner engineer, the inner parent, to become the best we can ever be on this journey we call life, we must make space for the silence. For it is only when we take the trouble to disconnect from external voices that we find the one voice that speaks only into the silence – the eternal spirit that dwells in each of us. Find that, and you begin to make your life into pure poetry.

The event finishes with more photo-taking by more cameras that I can number, accompanied by the signing of many autographs – on paper, on smartphones, even on flutes. But only two books are sold. Here, we are not among the soaring tower blocks and ubiquitous service coffee outlets of the metropolis. Resources here are more scarce and money is spent most carefully. It matters not to me. I am not here to sell books or to make money. Any money made will be left in this country, anyway. I am here to illuminate journeys. I can do that by speech and I can extend it by pointing those that want to know more to my website.

The second day's event is at Sinuknipan National High, but is attended by other schools in the district as well. Once again, we are out of doors, but screened from the intense heat by a roof over most of the audience. But there are many more here than it is designed to accommodate, so many are seated and standing in the sun. When we commence at 8:00 am, the heat is not as intense as yesterday, but still powerful enough to have the audience fanning themselves within a few minutes of becoming seated. This audience is a similar size but older – all appear around eighteen years or so. The event is billed as an extended workshop on creative writing. It will indeed cover this, but it must expand beyond the limits of that definition, to encompass all expressions of creativity. To me, there is no material difference in how that creativity expresses itself. Be it through music or home-making, poetry or policing, it is this creative spark that is the essence of our humanity. It is how we reflect the nature of the creator.

There is much final photo-taking and book-signing. All too soon, it is time to leave for the bus back into the city. We arrive at the bus station on time for the departure, only to discover that the 1:30 pm service left at 1:00 pm. So, we take the 2:30 pm bus, which naturally, pulls away at 2:15

pm, with maybe three occupants other than ourselves. I smile. This is the Philippines. We do things differently back in the UK.

An eight-hour journey lies ahead and this bus is of the stopping variety. Every few kilometres, sometimes less, it pulls over. It seems to be boarded and alighted by as many food and drink vendors as travellers. They purvey everything from bottled water and in-shell peanuts to chocolate bars. We will not go hungry. Amazingly, someone has packed a cheese sandwich for me. With this reminder of home, my thoughts turn to my nutritional journey, which for three years now, has been vegetarian. I have preliminary thoughts of progressing to a vegan diet and have so far commenced with a significant reduction in dairy intake. But though the logic of the step is obvious to me, the challenge is greater. And I wonder what I would do should there be future visits here, for these folk include flesh in almost all they eat. To decline also dairy products and all animal-based products would leave me, I guess, with very little to eat at all. But my weight management journey also has some distance to go, so perhaps, that would not be such a bad thing. I lose weight when in the Philippines anyway, and I am grateful to do so.

The kilometres slide under the bus as we climb into the cool of the mountains under a rainforest covering. The trees are of a different variety to those at home, but nevertheless, the spirits of the forest reach out to me in the same way as they do in my own New Forest back in the UK. The dryads are new, yet at the same time, familiar. I feel their welcome through the glass of the bus, for we are kindred spirits. I have said many times before that I number angels and dryads amongst my closest friends. People seem to think I am joking.

As the hour grows late, the sun leans out over the Pacific to be embraced back into a warm, welcoming sea. Eight hours later, we arrive in the city and are dropped, mercifully, only a thirty-minute taxi ride from my accommodation. This part of the city is still relatively undeveloped, at least by First World standards. Even at this time of night, it remains hot, the dust billowing all around us. This, too, is a city that never sleeps. Large numbers of people bustle around, pulling or carrying luggage as the never-ending traffic flows past on the elevated freeway above us. Small, unbranded retail outlets offer t-shirts, shorts, dresses and shoes in vast quantities for dramatically lower prices than I have seen in the shiny shopping malls further uptown. The sight has me wondering how many people have laboured, day after day, for who knows how many hours, in the back-street or upper-floor sweat shops to put these products on the street for such sums.

A taxi is summoned by smartphone and we watch its progress on Google Maps as it approaches. Even when it is only a matter of yards away, the system tells us to expect a further wait of almost twenty minutes, as it inches through the nose-to-bumper line of vehicles that stretches endlessly onwards into the night. The technology can tell us that the allocated minutes, hours and days of our lives are slipping silently away into the same darkness. It can do nothing to ease the endless human urge for motion, for transport, for the display of the badges of wealth and status by which we measure our self-worth on the human hierarchical scale.

At 10:30 pm, I drop gratefully into bed, but not before I have set the alarm for 3:30 am. At 5:30 am, I am due at the Eagles Broadcasting Studios for an appearance on national breakfast television.

Days 18–19:   Day Dream Believer

We arrive at Eagle Broadcasting at 5:00 am. I was interviewed on radio and Internet TV in these studios during my visit last year, but this is my first appearance on national TV anywhere in the world. This broadcast will reach out over a population now approaching a hundred million, so I am guessing the audience for this show numbers in millions. I find it hard to visualise what a hundred thousand people would look like, so yes, I am stepping once more into the unknown, into the Land of Risk. But unless I choose to dwell on those numbers, the risk is not daunting, for the studio is similar to the one I experienced last year. I know how to do this.

I am interviewed by Leo Martinez, Director of the Film Academy of the Philippines – and what a gentleman he is. He welcomes me and I respond, to his surprise and pleasure, with "Kumusta, Po." Foreigners don't often use Filipino, I gather. I know almost none. I never took to foreign language learning at school. I have often wondered if, later, I might have revisited that limiting belief. But though hearing technology has advanced at an astonishing pace during my lifetime, the cochlear implant has not restored a sufficient level of hearing to permit me readily to interpret the sounds and intonations of another language. Nevertheless, to me, a minimum mark of courtesy is to be able to say 'Hello' (Kumusta) in the language of the land you are visiting. And 'Po' is a term of respect, similar to 'sir'. I try to make a point of being able to say this, 'please', and 'thank you', in the language of any country I visit.

With an excellent connection achieved between us, Leo Martinez offers me full opportunity to talk about my work in the Philippines, my books and my website. Leo is a hugely accomplished high achiever. He feels no need to promote his ego and is generous in making much metaphorical space for me. My gratitude reaches out to him. I leave signed books as my only real means of thanks. Later, I will be told the Academy is looking for new material. What dreams may come?

The trip from my accommodation to the studio at 4:30 am took thirty minutes, much of it upon an empty freeway with eight lanes in each direction. The return at 6:30 am in the thick of the morning traffic takes two hours. I sit quietly as we crawl past the incongruous mix of shanty buildings contrasted against tall tower blocks, while from the billboards pale-skinned, airbrushed Filipinos exhort me to drink the right beer, wear the right clothes, live the right dreams – the ones that best stimulate our purchasing from the international corporations that pay the advertising agencies to make us want what they offer. And here, there is no less desire to live the dream than in the West where I live my dream. Because it is what we all want, isn't it?

Maybe, or perhaps, we only want it until we have squandered our time for long enough that we finally achieve some version of it, discovering how hollow it truly is. But by then, for most of us dreamers, it is too late. The hours and the days and the years have dripped through our hands like water and evaporated, never to return.

Taguig, Metro Manila: Economic miracle
or ticking time bomb?

With the rest of the day free, back in my temporary tower block home, I am intrigued to explore further the apparent economic miracle that is taking place around me. I visit the sales office responsible for marketing the apartments. Such sales are invariably off-plan, since all units scheduled to be completed within the next eighteen months have already been sold. I am informed that previous purchasers have seen the value of their investment double in four years. The implication is obvious: if I want to benefit similarly over the next four years, I need only to spend eleven million Philippines pesos on thirty-eight square metres in fashionable Bonifacio Global City (BGC) and happiness in the form of untold wealth and status can be mine.

But now, I am thinking at the macro level. For prices already to have doubled in the last four years, buyers now have to be found at twice the price that was asked four years ago. I am betting that local wages even in the metropolis have not doubled in that time. So, once again, for the most part, it is either going to be foreign investors or the local wealthy who are benefitting.

To understand why this is happening, we have to delve into the world of macroeconomics and international finance. Back in 2007–8, an economic tsunami surged across the globe, destroying banks and threatening to collapse the world financial system. The United States Federal Reserve Bank (The Fed) reduced US interest rates from 6.25% in July 2007 to an unheard of 0.5% in December 2008. The Bank of England, the European Central Bank and the Bank of Japan, to name just a few, followed closely behind. When that action, though historically unprecedented, proved insufficient to shock the financial heart of the world back into life, a vast quantity of electronic money was pumped into the international economy in the form of Quantitative Easing (QE).

By 2018, ten years on from the crisis, world economies have gorged on credit until they have become as bloated as sea-drowned cadavers. Yet, little of the money injected into the system has found its way into wages or production. Instead, it has gravitated to financial institutions and the wealthy, driving up stock markets to hitherto unknown multiples of corporate earnings, driving up the price of city housing, driving up personal debt to a level that is manageable only if interest rates stay at the lowest levels recorded in financial history.

But, at the time of writing, QE is being withdrawn and interest rates are rising, albeit, initially slowly. After ten years of ultra-low interest rates, large numbers of young borrowers have never experienced high interest rates. And now, the world is one heartbeat away from another financial cardiac arrest. As the Fed increases US interest rates, capital is already flowing out of developing economies back into the USA. The dollar is rising in value relative to other currencies. In many cases, those developing economies are obscenely over-borrowed in dollars – dollars that now cost far more in terms of their own currencies. Ultimately, such circumstances can have only one conclusion: financial devastation. If dollars pour out of the Philippines in the same way, real estate values in Manila will plummet, leaving the indebted incapable of repayment, or sustaining borrowing cost.

Across the world, real estate prices seem set to fall. In London and Sidney, they are already doing so. In some cases, perhaps universally, they will plunge. Past experience suggests that any recovery will be slow and painful, measured in years, not months. So, no, I do not spend eleven million pesos in pursuit of a financial dream built on slurry. And I fear for the financial future of many in this city who have already decided otherwise. This is how lives become blighted.

Saturday dawns in promising mode. Leo Martinez e-mails to say he is reading my short story collection, *The Goblin Child*, with the hope of seeing material suitable for film or TV. What dreams, indeed, may come.

This evening, we are due to head out of the city once more, this time to Ifugao, two hundred and twenty miles north of Manila, but still, over seven hours away by road. Whilst awaiting our chauffeur-driven transport, we dine sumptuously. For until you have eaten takeaway *lupiang sariwa* and *pancit* straight out of the container using a plastic fork, whilst seated in the waiting area of a Manila bus station, you cannot truly say you have experienced the Philippines.

Days 20–23:   I Dreamed My Dream for You

We arrive, a little dishevelled, at 5:00 am. The eight-hour bus ride was similar to the previous one but has entailed rather less sleep than I would have chosen. On arrival, I fall into bed, and fall immediately asleep. Four hours later,

I awake, shower (yes, hot water!) and head out to find something to eat.

We are staying in Poblacion, Alfonso Lista, in Ifugao. I am travelling this time with Prof. Pascual and Noah Ittangon, a young headmaster, who hails from these parts. Little is open today, it being Sunday. By way of explanation, my companions explain to me that most of the population here is Christian. I query this, since the Philippines seem to me to have an enormous Christian presence throughout. Clarification reveals that this area is Protestant. The distinction between Protestants who are Christians and Catholics, who, apparently, are not, intrigues me.

Breakfast, or lunch, or whatever it is at this time of the morning, is found in a small food court where most of the stalls are closed. I'm happy to settle for whatever is here, so long as it includes coffee. My meal is rice, bitter gourd and sautéed beans with pumpkin – unfamiliar, but much to my taste. Coffee is a sachet of instant Nescafé. Costa it is not, but it is hot and black and contains no sugar. That is quite an achievement here and is more than satisfactory.

I look out of the window at the concrete streets and see the ubiquitous cellphone much in evidence, along with many motorbikes and quite a few cars. Everywhere I have travelled in the Philippines, the cellphone is in evidence. Yesterday, when speaking to the Far Eastern University in Manila, I was told 90% of students have them. Here, I am guessing, it is rather less. But the phones and the stalls that sell them are very evident. They look incongruent to my western eyes, against a background of shanty homes, unpaved roads and unshod children. Available resources are spent on communication and transport in preference to accommodation and clothing. To some extent, this is to do with climate. For even at this higher altitude, the weather is still much like a summer day in the UK. However, I find myself wondering how many economic choices are being made on the basis of the urge to demonstrate status rather than the intrinsic worth to the purchaser. Young men will always want to display their rising level on the social scale through the ownership of transport, be it a Ferrari or a motorbike. Young women will always want to ride with the alpha male, and tell their friends about it by text and 'selfie'. Is that harsh? Sexist? Maybe so, but it is also a reasonable reflection based on a faithful report of observation. We do well to navigate political correctness with circumspection.

I muse upon the impact on formerly isolated communities of the tsunami of information that is the Internet. Back in Europe, we are inundated by a vast surge of incoming transient humanity, betting their luck against border guards and their lives against Poseidon, obsessed with dreams of a materially more comfortable life. The dream has been expertly crafted by western advertising agencies. Of course, if the urge were not there in us to have more appealing food, more possessions, more shiny promises of satisfaction, those ad agencies, and the TV and film promoters that depend upon and facilitate them, could not have built the foundation into the dream-edifice that soars above us today. But now, we do have it, such that it, too, has become a tsunami, a tidal wave of insatiable desire that strews the detritus of the discarded, material and human, over an undervalued planet.

Poblacion, Ifugao: old ways meet new

It will take most of us most of our lives to discover it is little more than a celluloid fiction, which distracts our attention away from achieving our own potential and outward, onto the sugar rush of unadulterated bling. By the time we discover that sugar rushes leave us unsatisfied, barely after the moment has passed, we will have squandered our most precious resource, our time, on the pursuit of airbrushed figments of someone else's imagination. If only I can have a cellphone, a car, more muscles, bigger breasts, more toys, more fame, more sycophants, more... something, then, I will be big. Then, I will be valuable. Then, I will be happy. Then, I will be loved. And thus, we stumble, blinded by neon, to the crematoria of squandered years, where we fall to our knees, weeping, as the scales fall from our eyes and ears as we acknowledge that the chance of deeper fulfilment has fled us by.

Sagely, we recycle diminishing planetary resources, for we are all eco-conservationists now. But when will we learn that the most precious resource of all, our time, cannot be melted down and recycled?

Monday dawns and I am preparing for a delivery to an audience of five hundred at Santa Maria National High School, Alfonso Lista. The upper half of the school will be attending, since, I am informed, creative writing is on the national curriculum. How very enlightened the curriculum designers must be! At breakfast, I ask Prof. Pascual to remind me of the name of the teacher who has invited us here. But she does not answer. I glance up to see that she has risen to her feet and is standing formally, her right hand upon her heart. We are just across the street from the town hall where the Filipino flag is being raised. In front of it is a gathering of perhaps a hundred and fifty public employees, standing to attention, singing the national anthem. I, too rise, in respect for the national identity of the country I am visiting. Later, I am informed that, quite apart from the inclination most feel to take pride in their country, there is a sanction for any seen to contravene: first, a reprimand, then community service, after that, fines and imprisonment. Non-compliance with that which is system-approved carries just as much of a penalty as it does in our culture.

We enter the school auditorium, a freestanding building at the centre of the town, to an audience that numbers over five hundred. Vertical iron girders support the structure's roof. Brick walls rise only to about two metres in height, the space between them and the roof being covered only with mesh, to prevent unauthorised entry, but open to allow air to circulate. Inside, the walls are stepped inwards, like in an amphitheatre, to create seating, auditorium-style. The space is half full, for it is capable of holding the whole school of a thousand pupils. Those before me are sixteen to eighteen years old, seated in horseshoe formation. The ends of the horseshoe extend beyond the table where I am seated, giving me an audience that stretches behind me, as well as to the front and sides. As normal, we commence with prayer and the national anthem. I take out my wallet, my mobile phone and my nervousness and put them down on the table. All are inconvenient when I speak.

I speak of comfort zones and the 'Journey to the Land of Risk' in search of the key that will open the cage in which is shackled the 'Poet', the spark of the divine who dwells inside each of us. I ask repeatedly, 'How far will you travel to find the key?' I quote T. S. Eliot: 'Only those who are willing to risk going too far can possibly find out how far one can go.' I speak of Odysseus and the Land of the Lotus Eaters, whose inhabitants lay in indolence. I quote

Homer, who has Odysseus chaining his sailors to the rowing boards to force them away. And there, in the auditorium with Odysseus, we 'smite the grey sea with our oars', as we flee sloth and self-doubt, committing ourselves to becoming the best we can possibly be.

For over an hour, there is barely a sound in this enormous space. Learning, together with its soulmate, opportunity, is highly valued here. Then, as I stop, the questions begin, only a trickle at first, for to speak up in front of five hundred of your peers is truly a step into the Land of Risk. How do I create such deep characters? They are all part of me. How could it be otherwise? Do I write for myself or others? I only write the words of the Poet who dwells within. If others have ears, let them hear.

As the questions grow in number, they delve deeper. How does one write a masterpiece? In response, I speak of Beethoven, of the impact of his impending deafness, of the temptation to stop when it becomes too hard, to settle in the Land of the Lotus Eaters. And all this for a man who had already written four astonishing symphonies and countless other brilliant works. As we consider this man's refusal to be thwarted, his cutting off of the legs from his piano to use the floor as a sounding board to create the fifth symphony, all become a huge metaphor for the creation of a masterpiece flowing from the Poet, the spirit inside.

Two hours later, we break. I wonder if they will all return. But after twenty minutes, not only are the seats all filled as before, still more people are arriving. Prof. Pascual takes over until the final hour, which is absorbed by yet more questions from these high-energy young people.

Then, it's lunch and I assume we are done. But no, we return for short stories from The Goblin Child and still more questions.

Housing on the road to Banaue is gradually being modernised

After seven hours of pouring forth unbridled energy, finally, we have to leave for Banaue. Today, I have learned something more about yielding freely to the Poet who dwells within. I have also learned much about what T. S. Eliot means when he says, 'Only those who are willing to risk going too far, can possibly discover how far one can go'.

Speaking of going far, Banaue is high in the mountains, another two-hour drive out from Manila, or I am told. Two hours, in the way of Filipino timekeeping, turns into three. As we rise on winding roads and hairpin bends, the air grows cooler and the engine of the minibus grows hotter. We stop frequently for the driver to spray the radiator and brakes from hosepipes provided at strategic points along the way. Evidently, it is not only our vehicle that has this problem. The concrete road, built as recently as 2010, periodically gives way to unpaved tracks, where landslides have taken the concrete. We pass houses clad with what I am informed is galvanised iron. The GI insulates from the cold. Many of the houses are of traditional design. Roofs are four-sided with sharp gradients rising to spire-like peaks. The buildings' footprints are maybe four metres by four. I am told that in these structures will live families with up to eight children. I visualise them piled to the roof, biggest at the bottom, smallest on top. I cannot be far wrong. Below the houses, tradition required that the dead be buried in seated posture. Connecting to your roots means something rather more literal here than at home. As we approach Banawe, it becomes evident that much modernisation is in progress and that gradually such buildings are being replaced. Soon, I guess, they will all be gone, consigned to The Museum of What the Ancients Did.

On reaching Banaue, we are accommodated in a hotel internally panelled with intricate carvings of pine, which grows freely here in the cool, dry air. We enter, of course, on the ground floor, at the front of the building. It is not until I head up for bed, I see that at the back, due to the gradient of the mountainside, that what at the front is the ground floor, at the rear is the fourth floor. I am wondering if we too shall sleep piled high, the littlest on top. If so, I would have to climb down several floors.

The following day is a day off. We squeeze yet again into a motorbike and sidecar, Noah riding pillion behind the driver. The space is tight, for I am not exactly diminutive. When they said they wanted a prominent poet from the UK, I don't think this was what they had in mind!

Banaue children

We stop for photos at a stall selling traditional clothing. Outside in the sunshine stands an elderly man, dressed in traditional costume, holding two spears for tourist photo opportunities. I am invited to dress in traditional costume. But I decline, for I do not care for imitation. However, I acquiesce to the persuasion of my fellow travellers to have a photo taken with the gentleman. He poses with his spear pointed to me and bids me do the same to him with the other spear. I do not want to participate in such a parody of violence. Instead, I point my spear up, away from him and take his hand, holding his eyes with my own. This elicits a broad, toothless smile of obvious delight. Cameras click. Namaste. I honour in this man that which is eternal. We give him twice the sum he asks for, in payment for the pictures. The labourer is worthy of his hire and this man will stand all day in the direct sunlight, for the whims of feckless tourists, many of whom will attempt to short-change him. I choose not be one. As the bike pulls us away, I am told I have made an old man very happy. "That's two of us," I think.

When travelling, it is wise to comply with local regulations

At the next stop, we have a photo opportunity spanning down a long, deep valley, which is carved much of the way up the mountainside with rice terraces. Covering almost four hundred square kilometres, the rice terraces are frequently referred to as the eighth wonder of the world. They took two thousand years to construct and were completed before the Common Era dating system began.

Standing all day in the sunlight for
the whims of feckless tourists

Here, we meet three Mormon missionaries. I initiate a conversation that I suspect most would avoid. They tell me that they are at the end of a two-year tour. Tomorrow, one returns home to Miami, another to New Zealand. I am introduced and my purpose in the Philippines explained. "How do you write poetry?" I am asked. This is probably the single most common question put to me when I am speaking publicly. The answer to these gentlemen is the same as I always give my audiences –"By connecting with the Poet, the spark of divine creativity that dwells in all of us, which we access in the silence."

Sufficient rapport has been created that they ask for details of my website. Though they use different metaphors and walk a nominally different path, the same spirit dwells in these men as does in me, even if they do not yet know it. We illuminate our roads by such light as is carried in the lanterns of our hearts.

As we talk, beside us squat six elderly ladies. These, too, are in regional costume, awaiting tourists seeking photo opportunities. One, who would be, perhaps, five feet tall if she could stand at full height, walks bent double, from the sun to the shade, barefoot and with faltering steps. I want to leave a gift with them. I want to meet and connect with them. I seek to shake hands with each. When I reach this particular lady, she does not offer her hand. All at once, it becomes obvious that she is blind. I reach out and touch her. "Kumusta. Salamat." (How are you? Thank you). It is all the Filipino I know. Like the gift I leave, it is not enough. It is never enough.

Tonight, we head back to the metropolis by ten-hour bus ride.

Day 25:   One Journey

De La Salle University's main campus is an oasis of calm in a city of movement. We allow two hours to cross this part of town from Bonifacio Global City (BGC) where I am staying, but in practice it takes only thirty-five minutes, such is the unpredictability of traffic in Manila. The lecture hall seats about two hundred, but seven minutes before we are due to start only twelve seats are filled. I am assured the audience will arrive. I assume we are on Filipino Local Time again. But no, students have classes some distance away. There are fifteen thousand students at De La Salle. They will get here when they get here – not all of them, I hope! We start on time to the usual prayer and national anthem, after which, young people continue to file in. They will continue to do so for the next forty minutes. There is an air of academic formality about the room. Tiered rows of seats, an AV system and fixed placed microphones, all contribute to the message that this is a place of formal learning. I am about to shatter the formality. Once introduced, I unwind the cable to free the microphone from its cradle and launch into the Land of Risk, pacing the room as I speak, often at volume.

The audience is restrained. I get the sense that whilst these guys will undoubtedly know what metaphor is, they don't 'get' metaphor, at least not emotionally. Eye contact is made, but there is a reluctance to connect emotionally. They have been taught, as I once was, to evaluate critically, to maintain emotional distance. It is a methodology that supports the gaining of an intellectual understanding of a subject. But it is not a strategy that engages the whole being – not one that sets the spirit free and lets the heart soar to become the very most we are capable of being. If we engage only with intellect, and neglect emotion and spirit, we grow lopsided. We can become intellectual giants, yet remain spiritual pigmies, our emotional intelligence stunted.

By the end, it is clear that something has resonated. Questions are deep and incisive, with no reluctance to step forward to engage. This is a hungry audience. And amongst them are young people whose hearts are already set on walking this path. One young man in particular asks repeated questions, even approaching me afterwards to explore our respective journeys in more depth. Later, in the university foyer, he will talk to me again, accompanied by a young woman. There appears to be an attachment. She has a different question. She is required by her course to make presentations but repeatedly freezes when doing so. Can I help? So, there, in the foyer, whilst awaiting the arrival of the taxi, we throw down the NLP (Neuro-linguistic Programming) Circle of Excellence and practise accessing resources she already has. She tells me she is relaxed and comfortable when reading. She can engender in herself the same comfort she feels in reading, when she is making presentations. Learning how to apply this single tool from NLP was a pivotal moment in my life. I have taught it and seen it employed with astonishing success, time after time. This young lady remains initially unconvinced of the power of what she has learned. If she utilises it when next presenting, she will be in for a pleasant surprise.

Returning to BGC takes more than two hours. Such is the unpredictability of the Manila traffic.

So now, my last presentation, for this visit, is done. I

have lost count of the number of events I have attended, the number of people I have connected with, the number of miles I have flown and travelled by bus. But numbers are only numbers. All they can do is calibrate. That calibration can offer a false sense of satisfaction, leading only to ego-building. 'I have sold x number of books. I have spoken to y number of people. I have made z number of foreign tours. And that must mean…' That must mean what? That I am a success? Success is a hollow nominalisation. That I am esteemed? Esteem evaporates in the heat of self-preoccupation. Let 'x' remain the unknown quantity of algebra. I am not here for enumeration or self-aggrandisement. I am here to shed light, such light as I have been given, in order to illuminate the journeys of others. As the quote on the wall of the teachers room at UMAK said, 'Teachers are like candles. They are consumed lighting the way of others.' In my turn, others have illuminated my journey before me, and to these I shall remain more grateful than I will ever be able to express. I will be a teacher for those who would learn of the One Journey that leads from the land of Comfort Zone where we sink into idleness, to the Land of Risk, where, by reaching further than indolence and procrastination believe we can, we rise to become what we were always meant to be, by discovering the divine spirit that dwells in each of us. The only number, the only calibration that matters, is how many days I have left in which to do this before I, too, return to my real home. And I am not speaking of the UK, for this is the journey, the One Journey that is life.

Stranger in paradise

Day 26: Stranger in Paradise

But it has been almost four weeks. My body is tired. The lovely people from the UCPE have arranged two days' recuperation at the beach. Tomorrow, we will head off to the Tamaraw Beach Resort at Puerto Galera on Mindoro Island. There's just one catch: I have to be up at 4:00 am for the bus!

The bus deposits us at the port for a one-hour sea crossing to Mindoro. As we file out of the terminal on the waterside, I assume we are making for the large sea cat docked just up ahead. But, no, we veer off to something rather smaller. In fact, if you were feeling uncharitable, you might think it reminiscent of a canoe, one that is covered, motorised, and seats fifty. I seem to be the only westerner on board. This might be a good sign. But then again, it might not. The gangplank is hauled aboard, itself an intriguing omen, and we depart. An hour later, the same gangplank is lowered and we descend direct onto the beach.

So, this is what paradise looks like. I had always wondered. The sand is warm to the touch and stretches up to a line of palm-shaded chalets, behind which is a large hotel building. The waves lap the shingle, as a cool breeze stirs the air. I am, at this moment, typing these words while seated on a raised thatched podium, looking out onto a deep blue sea. It is the perfect place for restoration. This has to be among the Philippines' best-kept secrets. Long may that remain the case; calibration numbs paradise.

In two days, I will take the thirteen-hour flight back to the UK and a small retired hearing dog, who has survived the cold and for now, outrun old age for another winter. Once through the terminal at Heathrow, I will be confronted by an icy wind and innumerable weary eyes that do not want to connect. I will smile and whisper to myself, "This is the UK. Back in the Philippines, we do things differently."

Mindoro Island, Philippines
March 2018

Journey's end – for now

If you have enjoyed and benefitted from reading 'One Journey',
would you please review it at Amazon?
This will help others find the book.
On Amazon, type: Michael Forester One Journey

**Thank you for reading *One Journey*.
I believe you will also value**

Forest Rain

Spiritual Learnings for a New Age

 Forest Rain is a collection of essays and verse, focussed on some of the main staging posts we pass through on life's journey.

Your spiritual journey is unique to you. But it is in mindfulness of the journeys of those who travel with us that we learn more of our own purpose and how we can draw energy and meaning from the challenges and events on our road.

This collection of Spiritual Learnings in prose and poetry forms a unique meditation that will support you in exploring your own journey, and the life events, both great and small, that will offer themselves to you as you travel forward.

These meditations will move you to joy; they will move you to tears. They will help you give yourself permission to experience the depth of learning to be found within, to experience fully what you have come into the world to learn and to teach. In so doing, they will support you in discovering the astonishing and profound messages meant for you alone, for *Forest Rain* truly is your Heart's Home.

To receive your copy of Forest Rain at a 40% discount, use the following discount voucher at Michael Forester's website.

Forest Rain Discount Voucher

**To receive your copy of
Forest Rain
at**

40% discount

visit
http://michaelforester.co.uk/books/forest-rain

At the check out page apply the coupon **one-journey**

Michael Forester will forward a signed copy of your purchase to you directly, dedicated in the wording of your choice.

If It Wasn't For That Dog

It's amazing what you can achieve with persistence, a bit of chopped liver and a second-hand teddy bear...

In 2002 Michael, a deafened man from the New Forest, lost his home, his marriage, his business and his father – but then again, he always was a tad careless. However, in the same year someone suggested that getting a dog might be a good idea – not just any dog, but a hearing dog from Hearing Dogs for Deaf People. And when, in 2004, Michael was presented with a Hearing Dog of his own called Matt, he just knew life would be so much easier. Amazing how wrong you can be, isn't it!

If It Wasn't For That Dog is the story of Matt's first year with Michael, the challenges and accomplishments of climbing the Hearing Dog learning curve, the profound changes he stimulated and the inestimable joy he confers magically on everyone who meets him. But most of all it is the story of the strange power of meaty treats to work miracles in doggie behaviour.

This book is available from my website at
www.Michaelforester.co.uk/books/if-it-wasn't-for-that-dog

Dragonsong

Sometimes nothing but the death of your father will do

Rebekah, noblewoman of Albion, has been driven to madness by the murder of her lover Vidar. In her torment she bargains with the Prince of Demons to turn her into a dragon. Thus transformed, she seeks to take revenge upon her father, Merlin, whom she is fooled into believing is responsible for Vidar's death. To save the world from the ravages of Dragonsong, Merlin is forced to banish his beloved daughter to hell, regardless of the consequences for him personally. Behind the subterfuge stands Oberon, Captain-King of Elves. He does not foresee the devastation his jealousy and unrequited love for Rebekah will unleash upon Gaia when he frees her from Merlin's spell and summons her from hell to support his war against Albion. To save Gaia a second time, Merlin is forced to travel back in time to prepare a warrior capable of overcoming the dragon through the power of the Sleep Stone. But he does not foresee the bond that will develop between the dragon and his own assistant, the Seer, Michael of Albion. If Lady Attie and Michael prove unable to return the Sleep Stone to the mouth of Hell in time, the Demon Army will swarm out of Hell and overrun Gaia. Time. Time is the key. Time is the only solution to Gaia's destiny – but only if the gods of Asgard can find a way to stop it.

This book is available from my website at
www.michaelforester.co.uk/books/dragonsong

The Goblin Child

Well, hello there.

Why don't you step inside and take a look round? You remember this place, don't you? That's right. You've been here before. And us, surely you remember us. We're old friends. This is where the light in your eyes glimpses the darkness in your mind.

Sit down and stay a while – if you can face the risk of finding out who you really are, that is. I'll introduce you to some friends of mine:

- Meet the man who remembers his birth. He wishes he didn't.

- And the goblin child – if his mother is to be believed.

- Or how about the boy who takes his god to school?

- Here's Madeleine, the author who can't get beyond chapter seven – because of the raven with white eyes, that is.

- And Santa. Yes, you really must meet Santa.

- But really it's all about David, who spent his life circling the moon – just like you and I do, in fact

Come with me. Come with me now.

This book is available from my website at
www.michaelforester.co.uk/books/the-goblin-child

A Home For Other Gods

Everything is under control

 It's 2117.

A country where everything you do has to be approved by the State; a State that tells you what to eat, when to shower, when to make love, what to think.

As the waters start to rise in the city, the fish people begin to arrive. Ultimately compliant, obedient without question, they open and close their mouths incessantly, saying nothing.

When Greg dares to think for himself, the Departmental Republic seeks to draw him into their elite to keep him quiet, to force his compliance. But if he agrees to be elevated to the level of the shadowy 'Gods,' it's going to cost him his home and the life of his family.

People are saying this ground-breaking novella reads like a follow-on to 1984.

This book is available from my website at
www.michaelforester.co.uk/books/a-home-for-other-gods

Vicious

A novel of punk rock
and the Second Coming

It's 2008. Tolly's a 40-something punk rocker who has always known Sid Vicious of the Sex Pistols would reincarnate to recommence their love affair. Now, she's met Henry, a 21-year-old student, she's convinced this is Sid, finally returned to love her forever.

Unfortunately, Henry has a girlfriend, Laura, who, to Tolly, is quite obviously the reincarnation of Sid's former girlfriend, Nancy Spungen. That can be sorted though. Tolly got rid of Nancy in 1978 (at least she thinks that's what she remembers doing) and she can do the same with Laura now. All she has to do is abduct her and make her remember how awful she was to Tolly in 1978.

This book is available from my website at
www.michaelforester.co.uk/books/vicious

Biographical

Michael Forester is a deafened writer who lives in Hampshire's New Forest with his hearing dog, Matt.

He can be contacted at
michaelforesterauthor@gmail.com

Michael Forester with hearing dog Matt.